THE DEADLY SILENCE

Hisham Mohammed

D1260976

THE DEADLY SILENCE

From the Devastation and
Hopelessness of War to a Journey
of Redemption and Peace

HISHAM MOHAMMED

With

G. ROSS KELLY

Gatekeeper Press™

Columbus, Ohio

The Deadly Silence

Published by Gatekeeper Press
2167 Stringtown Rd, Suite 109
Columbus, OH 43123-2989
www.GatekeeperPress.com

ISBN (paperback): 9781662906961
eISBN: 9781662906978

Dedication

This book is dedicated to innocent war victims
and peace loving people everywhere.

Contents

Part II: The Rest of the Story

Part III: Reflections and Reconciliation

Foreword

SEPTEMBER 11, 2001, was a very memorable day.
For those of us who lived in the United States, it felt
like some sickening combination of Pearl Harbor, the
assassination of JFK and the Oklahoma City bombing, all tied
together. Most Americans have very distinct memories of that
fateful day. If we were alive then, we know exactly where we
were. We were glued to our televisions as we watched replays
of the planes crashing into the twin towers in New York, the
plane crashing into the Pentagon, and the debris of the plane
that crashed in a field in western Pennsylvania.

We watched when each of the twin towers began to implode
and disintegrate to rubble. We watched in horror as the people
in New York ran aimlessly, breathlessly through the streets.
Those same streets an hour before had been filled with taxicabs,
pedestrians, and commerce. They were now filled with smoke,
ash, falling debris, and horrified runners, scrambling to find
safety. Around the country, we awoke to a beautiful, clear
autumn Monday morning. But by noontime, the serenity of
that morning had been shattered.

The memories of that day, and those that followed, are clear.

As the people in New York, Washington, and western
Pennsylvania began their recovery efforts, the rest of the

country, and perhaps the rest of the world, turned our attention to Washington.

President George W. Bush was in his first year as our president. His election victory over his opponent Al Gore the previous November had been extremely close and highly controversial. His victory, as opposed to it being a mandate by the citizen voters, was instead ultimately decided by the Supreme Court.

Bush had his supporters, but he seemed to have just as many detractors. There were questions about his intellect and his political savvy. His father, George Bush, Sr., who had been president just eight years prior, was aware of his son's critics and his liabilities. Perhaps it was for those reasons that he had advised his son to employ Dick Cheney as an advisor, to guide him through the murky waters of American politics. Cheney was a trusted carry-over from his own presidency, and the senior Bush felt confident Cheney could guide his son. Cheney had been Bush senior's secretary of defense during our country's initial war with Iraq, referred to as Desert Storm.

Cheney, in his first assignment to the new president, was asked to head up the search committee to name Bush's vice president. He found the perfect candidate . . . himself. The result was that during the initial months of the new president's tenure in office, Bush was viewed as no more than a figurehead. He was young, naive, and intellectually challenged, many thought. Cheney, many believed, was the real president. Bush was regarded somewhat as the president-in-training.

And now, after the events of 9/11, the eyes of the world were on the president. He would be tested like no American president since Franklin Roosevelt.

The young president came out swinging. We remember him standing in the rubble of the World Trade Center the day following the attacks. With one arm draped across the shoulder of a firefighter who had been working in the debris, Bush brashly declared over a megaphone his determination to avenge the attackers.

Osama bin Laden had already been known to the American people. Having proudly claimed responsibility for previous terrorist attacks against Americans, he was no stranger to Americans, and certainly not to the American intelligence community. Within hours of the attacks, it had already been determined that the events that had taken place were the work of bin Laden. He was the culprit.

But, bin Laden could not be found. He was in hiding, somewhere in the remote regions of Afghanistan or Pakistan. After Bush's brash declarations that those responsible for the horrid events would be captured and dealt with, it would not look good if he could not find bin Laden. Cheney convinced Bush that there was another, perhaps more expedient, option. If we couldn't capture Osama bin Laden, perhaps we could make Saddam Hussein our culprit. Bin Laden could not be found; Saddam Hussein could. And, Cheney and Bush had it in for Hussein from the last war.

The propaganda began.

We were told Hussein had sinister plans for the United States. We were told he was stockpiling weapons of mass destruction, which became normalized in our vocabulary as WMDs.

We were told by Bush and by Vice President Cheney it was not a question of *if* Saddam possessed WMDs, but where he was hiding them. We were told how Hussein was acquiring yellowcake uranium, an ingredient necessary for the development of nuclear weapons. We saw Colin Powell, the retired general who had served admirably in the previous Gulf War and was now Bush's ambassador to the United Nations, obediently follow the script by echoing the same points against Hussein to the United Nations.

Bush not only had the U.S. Congress and the majority of American people convinced, but he now had many of the world's leaders behind him. Osama bin Laden was clearly the mastermind of the events of 9/11, but Saddam Hussein was somehow the culprit. If we could not find bin Laden, we must take action against Hussein. The case was made, and the world bought it.

You were either "with us," Bush told the world, or "against us."

Following Bush's initial pronouncements, the public face of the subsequent series of events was that of Bush's secretary of defense, Donald Rumsfeld. On a near-daily basis, Rumsfeld took the television podium to explain how, if Hussein failed to comply with the U.S.'s ultimatums to relinquish his WMDs, Iraq would encounter a "shock and awe" military assault, the likes of which he and his country would not survive. Rumsfeld described in infinite detail the overwhelming military power that would be deployed against the country.

To allay the fears of those who decried that the assault Rumsfeld described would result in massive civilian casualties, the defense secretary confidently countered by describing new, more precise technologies. We would use ordinance referred to as "smart bombs," which could be deployed with pinpoint precision.

Rumsfeld enjoyed the spotlight. He was almost gleeful about the new toys his forces would deploy. His claims were illustrated with videos of bombs being dropped down chimneys of buildings, or onto buildings next to residential areas that were untouched by the blast.

Whether it was reality or a masterful job of video manipulation, the public bought it. A war against the world's most heinous villain, other than Osama bin Laden, would be executed with minimal civilian casualties. The assault would target only the forces of Hussein.

This was the perspective from inside the U.S.

We didn't know what Saddam Hussein's role was in the events of 9/11, if any. We didn't know if he was developing weapons of mass destruction or not. The Bush Administration certainly thought so. But in the U.S., there were many who thought the administration was misguided. Why go after Saddam Hussein? Bin Laden was the guy we wanted. But they prevailed.

Bin Laden was nowhere to be found, and Saddam Hussein was considered just enough of a bad actor by the Americans, and he *could* be found. In the eyes of many Americans, he became the villain of choice until the real villain could be found.

Years earlier, Hussein had attempted to invade neighboring Kuwait. That effort had been successfully thwarted by Bush's father, George H.W. Bush, when he was president. That victory over Hussein, though, was not without consequences. Bush, Sr., we were told, supposedly suffered countless humiliations and assassination attempts by Hussein and his henchmen before it was over. Perhaps the treatment of his father by Hussein also played into the younger Bush's and Cheney's obsession with the hated Iraqi leader. Whatever it was, and whatever the justification, valid or not, the "shock and awe" campaign commenced as advertised in and around Baghdad on March 20, 2003.

To those of us who were not directly affected, this was a distant war. It was happening in a far-off place against a leader we were told we should despise. To those of us not in the line of fire, this was a war to be watched on television. It could have been a reality show or a series. We could watch the nightly explosions and the U.S. military humvees patrolling the streets of Baghdad. Or, we could watch the events unfold on the nightly news, or read about them in the morning paper.

That is, for those of us who were not directly affected.

For those who were affected, it was a much different war. Thousands of Americans fought and died in that war. Thousands more were wounded or dismembered. Today, more than a decade later, many veterans suffer from the horrors of that war with missing limbs and worse. And even more were affected by the traumas of the war, suffering from what is referred to as post-traumatic stress disorder, or PTSD, another acronym that has since become a part of our lexicon.

Even today, veteran suicides are commonplace across the American landscape. Ask any individual or family who was affected by the war against Saddam Hussein if it was a television war.

And that is just the American perspective. Contrary to the many pronouncements about "smart bombs" and minimum civilian casualties, thousands of Iraqi civilians were equally, if not more, affected. This was their country we invaded. These were their homes and neighborhoods.

Buildings and institutions were destroyed. Monuments that had stood as religious and historical landmarks for thousands of years were reduced to mere rubble. More significantly, thousands upon thousands of Iraqi citizens were killed, maimed, or displaced. Families were separated and destroyed. Countless lives were altered in ways many will never know or truly understand.

One of those lives was that of an 8-year-old Iraqi boy named Hisham Mohammed.

As we watched the war unfold on CNN, Hisham was living with his family in the Iraqi town of Ramadi, about 110 kilometers west of Baghdad. In the earliest days of the war,

Ramadi was on the fringes of the fighting. The real focus was Baghdad and other strategic strongholds around the country. But as the fighting progressed, it began to reach outlying areas such as Ramadi. There was a military installation nearby. Instead of watching the war, Hisham and his family were now in it—but still somewhat on the periphery.

Until that day.

On the morning of March 22, 2006, Hisham, his friends and brothers were playing outside their home. Without warning, there was a massive explosion. A friend was killed. Two of his three brothers were injured. But it was Hisham who endured the brunt of the blast more so than his brothers. His spinal cord was severed by the blast. Not knowing if he would survive, or even if he had already died, neighbors hurled the three boys into their vehicle and navigated the war-torn streets to get them to the hospital. It was then that Hisham's parents discovered the horror that had befallen their sons.

Hisham's parents worked at the hospital as physicians. They saw injured civilians brought into the hospital every day. They treated war injuries daily. And, as physicians are trained to do, they treated them with compassion, but they had to maintain an objectivity about their work so as not to be emotionally overcome by the sheer horrors of their jobs.

This day, however, would be different. This time, they encountered a horror only a parent can know. This time, the lives of Hisham and his family would be altered forever. While the other brothers would recover, Hisham was rendered completely paralyzed.

Their efforts to secure the treatment their son would require from the events of that day would take them on an around-the-world odyssey. From their hometown of Ramadi, they would travel to the capital city of Baghdad, to the country of Jordan, to Russia, and eventually to a Shriners Hospital in the United

States...the very country that inflicted this life-altering tragedy.

At some point in our lives, most of us endure some sort of change that requires us to adjust and to redefine who we are. Loss of a job, a divorce, an illness, or any number of life events can force us to change our direction. That usually happens later in life. But in Hisham's case, he was forced to redefine who he was at the age of eight.

Today, Hisham Mohammed is 23 years of age. He now resides with his family in the suburbs of Philadelphia, Pennsylvania. He remains fully paralyzed. Despite all they have endured, Hisham and his family have resurrected their lives in the very country that had destroyed their previous life. Through their faith, their determination, their loyalty to one another, and their hard work, they, as Iraqis, have much to teach us about who we are as a country. They are the embodiment of the American dream.

Their goal and their message are one and the same: to serve as a living testament to the horrors of war; to help others who suffer, be that from war, domestic abuse, or any other of life's traumas; and, to personify the lyrics of the song written for Nelson Mandela, *Nine Thousand Days* . . .

> *It matters not the circumstance.*
> *I rise above; I took a chance.*

For Hisham, he and his family have moved past that horrific day in 2006. Without the use of either his arms or legs, and with the endless help of his family, he has navigated from a near-death experience to now reside in the very country that inflicted that near-death experience. He and his family hold fast to the goal of integrating themselves into their new country and being agents of change for peace.

What seems impossible to most of us has become a mere matter of principle and conviction to this Iraqi-turned-American family. What is it that resides in this family and that most of us simply don't possess? Theirs is a story of unyielding courage, determination, and conviction.

Some characterize the story of Hisham and his family as one of political intrigue and the most horrendous effects of war. But it is so much more. It is a story of the strength and power of the human condition to overcome the most outlandish of indescribable events. It is the ultimate story of will, perseverance and faith. Theirs is a story of the ultimate do-over.

As the ancient scribes once told us, *That which resides in some is beyond the comprehension of many.*

Here, in his own voice, and with the help of his family on those occasions when his voice had been silenced, is Hisham's story.

—G. Ross Kelly

Prologue

I‌T IS GENERALLY thought that the initial sensation of an explosion is a deafening roar followed by a devastating concussion, reducing its recipients into semi-conscious, limp and lifeless forms of debris and rubble. The reality, in contrast, however, is that preceding the ear-shattering noise and the annihilating destruction, there was an ever-so-brief moment when eyes were locked together, thoughts were frozen in wonder, and the environment became totally void of oxygen, leaving nothing but to be paralyzed in an eerie, deadly silence.

That brief moment of confused wonder was followed by an explosion that struck four brothers, all narrowly escaping death, one completely paralyzed, and a once-prosperous family completely uprooted to an around-the-world saga and the creation of a new home—leading them, in fact, to the very country that was instrumental to their destruction in the first place.

"The Deadly Silence" is the story of that devastating day, and more remarkably, the incredible journey that followed.

Introduction

As Iraqis, we had grown accustomed to conflict. As far back as the Iran-Iraq War in the 1980s, Iraq was at war. Then came the invasion of Kuwait and the war known as Desert Storm that followed. We were accustomed to turmoil.

However, despite being constantly at war and being subjected to the political sanctions and shortages that accompany war, my father had a clear vision of what he wanted for himself, for my mother, and for my three brothers and me.

Me with my brothers, in our earliest days. From left, my oldest brother, Mohammed, holds Ali, and Mustafa holds me at our home in Ramadi, Iraq, circa 1999.

For starters, that included remaining in our home in Ramadi. He and my mother were both physicians. They would continue to cultivate their medical practices, his specializing in the treatment of allergies and hers specializing in ophthalmology, and they would raise and educate me and my three brothers. Each of the four of us would complete our educations and pursue our own professions. We would marry and raise our own families. And we would live together in a multi-story compound. We would have our own living quarters, but we would remain together, as a family.

His vision was clear.

And he had us all marching toward that vision. My Dad and Mom were thriving in their respective medical specialties. Each of my brothers was progressing nicely in school. And I, as the youngest of the brothers, was doing all I could to keep up with them.

Me with Ali, at home in Ramadi in 2000.

We were all enjoying school. We were active in sports and enjoying our time with our friends. And we were doing so in the home that was to be our family residence where we would all one day reside. All was progressing nicely and according to plan . . . until that day.

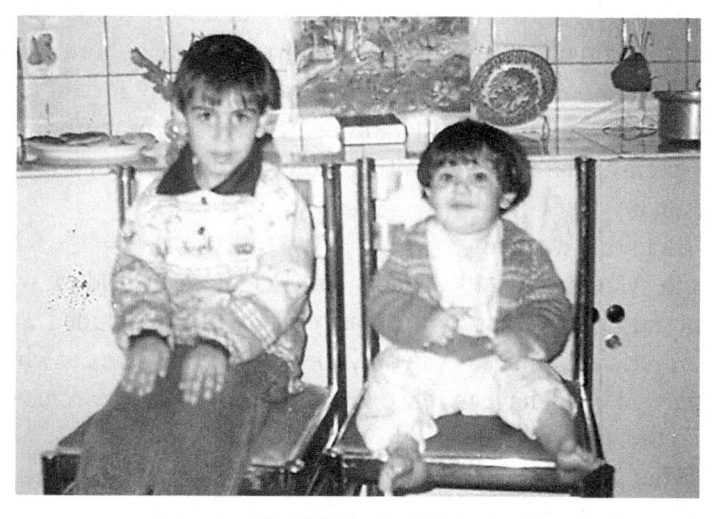

Ali with me in 2001.

We had grown accustomed to political turmoil in our country. Before I was born, there had been the decade-long war with Iran. Then there was the initial war with the U.S. in the 1990s, referred to as Desert Storm. Then there was the second war with America in 2003, which became catastrophic for me and my family. I was a child and felt somewhat insulated from the conflicts, though I'm sure my family was feeling the effects of the war. The U.S. had imposed sanctions on our country. Medical supplies were not as plentiful. There were food shortages. There were no-fly zones that restricted travel.

Buildings were destroyed. Religious artifacts that had stood for ages were destroyed. Foreign troops were in our country in search-and-destroy mode against any and all forces that were loyal to Hussein. Local militia groups were in search-and-destroy mode against the American invaders. As innocent bystanders, all we could do is watch the various factions kill each other and destroy our country in the process.

Eventually those search-and-destroy missions found their way to Ramadi. We watched in horror as neighbors were harassed and even killed . . . sometimes by enemy forces, and sometimes by local militia for being accused of harboring the enemy. The war was getting closer to us and much more personal.

Then, that day came.

On March 22, 2006, I was only eight years old. I was knocked unconscious by the blast that we had concluded was an American bomb, so I can only speak directly to parts of what happened. I will have to rely on my brothers and my parents to fill in the details.

What I do know is that, in the blink of an eye, the entire focus of our family shifted from my father's original vision, one of pursuing our own lives in the country we loved, to one of an around-the-world journey of survival and recovery.

This is my story.

PART I

Hisham's Journey

CHAPTER 1

A Rumbling in the Distance

OUR HOME IN Ramadi was about an hour away from Falluja and about two hours away from Baghdad. As the war began, America had its sights set squarely on Saddam Hussein and anything related to him. Unfortunately, one of his homes was in Ramadi, which eventually put our hometown in the crosshairs of the conflict.

Life was becoming dangerous in Ramadi. We had learned to live with the unsettled realities that leaving your house meant you may not come back, and going to sleep at night meant you may not wake up. Gunshots and bomb explosions were commonplace, as were unannounced raids on our house in the middle of the night. American troops were in a continuous search for weapons and militia insurgents. I remember nights when we would be awakened at gunpoint and forced to wait outside our home, sometimes until sunrise, or whenever the search was over.

Throughout the city, there were occurrences of people being killed, injured, or kidnapped, either by American soldiers or by Iraqi insurgents, who targeted them because they were suspected of cooperating with the Americans. Bomb explosions were growing more and more constant. We were now in a war zone and forced to live with an increasingly scary and disruptive situation.

My mom remembers the troops looking for insurgents in other places, even hospitals. It wasn't unheard of for them to bust into sterile operating rooms. Teachers were killed. Doctors were killed. Other professionals and civilians were killed.

Some died at the hands of soldiers fighting a war, others at the hands of militias that seemed to come out of nowhere, taking advantage of a war-ravaged land to spread their message of death.

Those times when our home was invaded, my parents would politely comply with the Americans, but at the same time, try to reason with them. As physicians, both of my parents had learned English, so they were able to communicate with the Americans. They were not insurgents, nor were they hiding insurgents, my father would tell the soldiers. They were physicians.

I can remember my mother lecturing the Americans, telling them that if they were attempting to win the hearts and minds of the Iraqi people, they were going about it the wrong way. She would invite them in for food and drinks in hopes of convincing them to stop kicking our door down and pointing weapons at her young sons. My parents would leave notes on the front door, or even provide the troops keys to our home to minimize the damage from their invasions.

Even though I was very young at the time, I have a memory of American troops directing their weapons at us kids during one of their late-night surprise raids. We were kids. What did they think we were going to do? Were we somehow threatening?

I didn't think so, but who knows what goes through the minds of soldiers in the midst of battle?

I can still see the boot marks on the walls and doors of people's homes, and images of the soldiers hopping exterior fences, pounding on doors and yelling for homeowners to open up. I remember my father trying to reason with the American troops. We had nothing to hide, he would tell them. We didn't have weapons. We weren't a threat. There were occasions when we would see the same troops over and over again. Yet our front door continued to get broken. My young mind at the time simply couldn't comprehend these late-night raids and why troops carried them out the way that they did.

But the invasions continued, and the tactics remained the same. The Americans trusted no one. In their eyes, Iraqi insurgents could be anyone and anywhere. The insurgents, on the other hand, would kill, injure, or kidnap any Iraqi they thought was cooperating with Americans. We were simply an Iraqi family caught in the midst of deadly competing forces. Trying to live a peaceful life under those circumstances was not an easy thing to do. But my parents were determined.

In the midst of the environment of mistrust and violence, however, I remember my father and one American soldier having a conversation that went a little differently than many of the typical interactions. The American said that he did not want to hurt civilians, and that he only wanted to make sure his team was safe and protected. He was very polite and honest with my dad. They both spoke in English.

The soldier further confided in my father that he only wanted to finish up his tour so he could safely return home to his people. It was a sentiment that my father could relate to. After all, we are all about family, and it wasn't hard for us to understand this man's concerns and desires.

That was one of the many paradoxes of the war.

Another was the conflicting views of Saddam Hussein. To the Americans, and perhaps the rest of the world, Saddam Hussein was an evil despot who needed to be eliminated. They, we were told, were determined to save us from his sadistic tyranny.

By contrast, the people of Iraq actually felt safe during Saddam's reign. When he was in power, there were no terrorists. There was little crime to speak of, and people felt safe in their own homes and communities. Further, we had free health care and free education. Our lives were basically good, as long as we did not interfere in the country's politics.

But in the Americans' efforts to eliminate our terrible despot and save us, they created an atmosphere of terrorism and fear that we had not previously known. And all the while, the soldier told my father, the troops who were sent to save us and our families only wanted one thing . . . to get back home safely to their families.

Oh, the ironies of war.

As time went on, as the war became more and more entrenched into our daily lives, the events became more personal for us. At his clinic, my father worked with a fellow doctor who was a Christian and feared staying in Ramadi because of religious persecution. He planned to sell his medical practice and move to a different part of the country, one where a Christian could live in peace.

Neither my father nor his coworkers or people in the community cared that the man was a Christian. The local militia insurgents, however, did care. The doctor had found a buyer, sold his practice, and was preparing to move. On the day of his planned move, however, he was shot and killed inside of his clinic.

This incident was hardly isolated during these early years of the war, as many others, professionals included, were killed for their religious beliefs. Religion was at the very core of the war. Americans wanted to "save" us from the evil Saddam Hussein, and different militia groups had different agendas. Some targeted Christians and others targeted Sunni or Shia Muslims. In the end, no one was safe.

Once, while praying at a local mosque, we were given a flyer that had been left outside warning against talking or cooperating in any way with the Americans. This was just another way for the militia to remind and put fear into people. While we were very afraid of these militias, we didn't really know who they were or where they came from at that point in time. We simply called them militias. They later would call themselves Al Qaeda.

Through it all, however, we still persevered, determined to live our lives, working and going to school as we would at any other time. There were days when we were forced to flee our school due to gunshots, but we continued our education. There were days when my dad would come home very late due to being trapped in his afternoon clinic to help his patients. And despite all the risks of traveling, we still visited our extended family in Baghdad and Babel.

War was our new reality. But we continually tried to look for ways to enjoy the simple pleasures of life. For my brothers and me, that meant playing and having fun with neighbors and friends. For our family, it meant visiting friends and family, worshipping, and enjoying our time together. We were devoutly religious and extremely close as a family, and it is those two factors that helped us maintain our sanity after the war had begun.

Whatever the politics, whatever the outcome, our goal was to remain as far removed as we could from what was taking place around us.

If only we could have known what awaited us.

CHAPTER 2
March 22, 2006

F OR AMERICANS, WHEN the Japanese attacked the U.S. naval base at Pearl Harbor in Hawaii at the beginning of World War II, President Franklin Roosevelt said of the following day, "December 7, 1941, a date which shall live in infamy."

The date which shall live in infamy for my family and me is March 22, 2006.

Our parents, both physicians, were at work in the local hospital on that date, and the four of us boys were at home, waiting to attend our afternoon school session. During those times, the boys and girls attended school separately, rotating between morning and afternoon sessions. On this particular day, we were scheduled to attend the afternoon session.

It was a sunny day and already getting warm. My oldest brother, Mohammed, was 16. Mustafa, the second oldest, was 14. Ali, the third oldest, was just short of his 12th birthday. And I was 8. Being the youngest, I always had to work hard to keep up with my brothers. Fortunately, I was scrappy and fast . . . perhaps the fastest of the group.

We loved playing outdoors with our neighbors. Whether it

was football (soccer to Americans), or any type of childhood game, we were all active and always having fun.

The day was rather unremarkable. I remember it starting out as a beautiful, sunny day, but eerily quiet.

On that morning, my three brothers and I were outside hanging out with our friends until it was time for our school session to start. We were now living in a war zone, and given the activity that was taking place in the area, we were actually discussing if it would be safe to go to school that day.

That moment will be forever vividly entrenched in my mind.

I was standing with my back up against the wall of our neighbor's home as we talked. My leg was propped up against the side of the house, and I was talking with the others about nothing in particular. That's when I heard it . . . a strange whistling sound off in the distance. I remember asking the guys if they had heard something. Before they answered, I began getting a ringing in my ears.

That was the last moment of my life that I would have as a playful, rambunctious child, able to walk by my own power. The next sensation I remember was that of being catapulted through the air.

During that time, American soldiers had concluded that Iraqi insurgents had taken over some territory in our home city of Ramadi. During that time, it was not uncommon for us to find ourselves in the midst of firefights between the two forces. Evidently, that morning, an attack was being launched by the Americans to root the insurgents out. Unfortunately, my brothers, neighbors, and I were caught in the crossfire.

That shrill whirring sound was what preceded an explosion from a mortar shell that landed in our street. When the explosion hit, everything went dark. I was catapulted through the air by the blast, and I remember landing on a curb, and then crying out for my mom and dad. I was crying out, but no sounds were coming out of my mouth. I was awake but in a state of shock and unable to move or speak. I was also having trouble breathing. I remember trying to say something to my brothers but not being able to.

When I landed from the force of the explosion, my head hit the curbing of the street. My body and limbs were littered with shrapnel wounds from the blast, and my head was equally bloody from landing on the curb.

My brothers Mohammed and Ali were also injured. Mustafa, my second-oldest brother, was uninjured during the incident, having been luckily shielded from the shrapnel by the power of God.

It finally dawned on me that I was unable to speak. Whatever it was I was trying to communicate with my brothers was lost in my inability to formulate words. I tried to move my body but could not. I was motionless and speechless, and my eyes were a blur. I could make out the images of my brothers, but everything was out of focus and seemed to be happening in slow motion.

I could feel my brother Mohammed picking me up and moving me towards our house. My brother Mustafa was assisting Ali, who was also injured. Mohammed, who too was injured, placed me on the ground in the garage of our house. I was bleeding from my neck and my brothers tried to stop it with cotton as best as they could. I remember gasping for air and feeling in a daze. I was in a pool of my own blood, which was gushing from my neck.

I was in a state of shock, and by this time was fading into unconsciousness. My brother Mustafa, who was the only one of us not injured by the blast, was in the unfortunate position of having to witness the chaotic scene. I had to rely on him to describe the events that followed.

According to Mustafa, seeing my condition, my brothers

began crying out for help. Thankfully, our neighbors came to our aid. They loaded us into a van to transport us to the hospital. I was told their greatest concern at the time were the injuries suffered by Mohammed and Ali. I was lifeless and presumed dead, so they placed me into the back of the vehicle, where I was accompanied by Mustafa. He described looking into my open, lifeless eyes, and continually saying to me, "You will be OK. You will be OK."

In contrast to his reassurances, all indications were that I would not be OK. The early assumption was that I had died from the blast.

During times of emergencies, all hospital staff are alerted and trained to provide any assistance they can. In this situation, hospital staff members, including my parents, had been alerted to the explosion and were mobilized to assist incoming patients.

Unknown to us, prior to our arrival, our father was already busy treating patients, including three of our friends who had also been injured by the blast. Two of them had suffered minor injuries to their legs. The third, however, was more serious.

Our friend was 12 years old. As we later learned, he had been severely wounded by shrapnel from the explosion. In a state of shock, he had picked himself up after the explosion and begun to run frantically, holding his hand against the wounds to his chest to slow down the bleeding. When he had stopped running, he released his hands from his wounds, causing the blood to spew uncontrollably. The shrapnel had penetrated his heart.

As we learned, he continued to run towards his house but collapsed. His brother had prepared to lift him and have him taken to the hospital, but he told his brother he knew he was dying and not to subject himself to further risk. His only request was to see his mother.

Despite his protests, they did take him to the hospital, and he was being treated by my father. The boy was right. He was dying anyway. Those words to his brother were his last.

When we arrived in the midst of what was already a chaotic scene in the emergency room, Mustafa saw another friend of ours crying and banging his head against the wall in anguish. He asked him what had happened. It was then that Mustafa learned that our friend had died.

I was later told that our neighbors who had brought us to the hospital were screaming for someone to help us. My brothers, Mohammed and Ali, were placed on stretchers and were being cared for by nurses. Mustafa remained with me. I was not being tended to, again because the assumption was that I had died from my wounds.

As Mustafa later told me, it was our father who was the responding physician as he approached the area, and seeing Mustafa, he asked, "Why are you here?" According to Mustafa, he responded by pointing to the three of us and saying, "My brothers." My father immediately checked on Ali and Mohammed, and both were being treated and appeared to be out of imminent danger. He then focused his attention on me.

My brother Mohammed had taken shrapnel from the explosion, which had injured his back and legs. My brother Ali had suffered serious injuries to both legs, and he had not realized this until he saw blood running down his leg and onto his thobe, which is traditional Arabic clothing. Fortunately, the treatment they would require for their wounds could be provided in Ramadi.

Hisham, Mustafa told my father, is the one who needs your help.

Having already dealt with the trauma of watching our friend die, then seeing Mohammed and Ali, and then me, I can't imagine what emotions our father was feeling. He knew something was terribly wrong and immediately went into doctor mode. But this time, it was not our friend's son . . . it was his own.

In a way perhaps more devastating than we will ever know, my father, as a medical doctor and a parent, was put to the ultimate test. He had to maintain the stoicism and objectivity of a physician, while two of his own sons lay injured and a third was presumed dead. How he remained strong enough to stay in doctor mode can only be a testament to God and his strong faith.

After examining me, my father realized I was still very much alive. He discovered a light pulse. He stopped the bleeding and arranged to have me taken to the operating room to ligate the bleeding blood vessel. Also, I had lost a large amount of blood from the explosion and required a blood transfusion.

When I woke up, I was in the intensive care unit of the hospital and hooked up to numerous machines. I was unable to move or speak and was having difficulty breathing. But I was alive.

Within hours after our arrival at the hospital, it was concluded that Mohammed's and Ali's injuries could be treated there. It was concluded that mine could not. We would later learn that the shrapnel from the explosion had severed my spine; however, at the time, the doctors were unsure of what was causing these issues. And given the limited medical capabilities in Ramadi, they were unable to diagnose the situation further.

They advised my father to transfer me to Baghdad, which was some two hours away. And that was on a good day, under normal conditions.

Through all of the bedlam that had taken place, my mother had also come to the emergency room only to see the horror of three of her sons on stretchers. Her first reaction was the reaction I think any mother would have in that situation. She broke down crying and was taken to a side room by one of her colleagues to gain her courage and her composure. As she returned to find my father caring for me, I was told, she devoted her attention to Mohammed and Ali. While their wounds could be treated locally, I would learn, mine could not. As I was barely conscious, my parents and brothers had some difficult decisions to make . . . and quickly.

My situation would require me to be transferred to Baghdad, Iraq's capital city and a place that offered better medical care. But we were in the midst of a war. Supplies were scarce. Vehicles were scarce. Resources were scarce. We would be going into a war zone with roadblocks and checkpoints and the risk of gunfire.

Those were all issues my 8-year-old mind, especially in the condition I was in, could not comprehend, but issues my family was confronted with at the time. Nor did I realize at the time that this day would be the last time I would see my home, the last time I would see my friends, the last time I would do any of the things I could do when I woke up that morning.

And at a time when I wanted to feel the warmth and togetherness of my family, my father and I would be embarking out into a war zone on our own . . . without the comfort of my mother and my three brothers.

I would later realize we were not just going to another hospital in Baghdad; we were saying goodbye to the life that we had woken up to that morning, never to see it again.

The journey of our new life, yet to be defined, was just beginning.

CHAPTER 3

55 Days in Baghdad

THIS WAS NOT a good time to be taking a road trip from Ramadi to Baghdad. The capitol city was the epicenter of the war, and the route would be littered with skirmishes, firefights, checkpoints, and roadblocks. The Americans were focused on flushing out militia militants and had checkpoints throughout the area to find them. They made no distinction in their searches between the militants and innocent Iraqi civilians. As far as the Americans were concerned, we were all the same, and now we would be moving right into the heart of the battleground.

But my situation was critical, and Baghdad was the place my father felt we had to be. And he was determined to get us there. But he would need help. He needed an ambulance and someone to drive while he watched over me during the trip. Miraculously, he was able to secure both. He was able to obtain an ambulance from his hospital, and a friend volunteered to accompany us on the risky journey, war or no war. My father had a critically injured son and was prepared to spare no expense or no indignity to get me where he felt I needed to be.

I can only imagine what that day was like for him. As a physician, he was called on to help with the injuries and casualties that had occurred as a result of the bombing. The shock and sadness of watching one of our friends die amidst the chaos must have been unbearable, only to then experience the shock of seeing his son, Mustafa, standing there in the emergency room informing him of his three injured brothers, one of whom had been presumed dead.

That day was tragic for all of us. We lost our home and the life we once enjoyed. Two of my brothers were injured. After the immediate treatment necessary to keep me alive, it was determined that my recovery could not be achieved in Ramadi, but had to be pursued elsewhere. And, somehow, through it all, my father maintained his resolve, all while dealing with the anguish of having three of his four sons injured, and one near death. Yet, his day was far from over.

My mother would be left in Ramadi with Mustafa to care for my two other brothers, Mohammed and Ali.

With the hastily arranged plan in place, my father and his friend prepared to set out for Baghdad. I was unconscious during the entire trip. My father was focused on getting me to Baghdad for treatment, war or no war.

I would later learn that the trip was filled with delays and obstructions from the very beginning. What would have ordinarily been a two-hour journey took more than six hours. There were checkpoints, roadblocks, and vehicle searches at virtually every turn, and each was scrutinized and cross-examined with the same series of questions: Who were we? Why were we traveling?

Were we Al Qaeda? Were we hiding weapons or Al Qaeda in our vehicle?

The fact that we were traveling by ambulance and that I was obviously in critical condition did little to spare us from the scrutiny. The Americans took no chances. They were suspicious of everyone and were conditioned to expect the worst from the least likely sources ... women, children, the infirm, or even a catastrophically injured 8-year-old boy trying to get to the hospital for life-saving medical care.

No one was exempt.

I was told that some of the soldiers were more sympathetic to our situation than others. I remember one who had a bomb-sniffing dog and who was kind enough to instruct the other troops to let us pass through the checkpoint after he had spotted me in the vehicle. I must have really appeared that bad.

An Ambu bag, a device my father used to keep me breathing during our trip to Baghdad.

Throughout the journey, we were completely cut off from my mother and three brothers. There was no reliable cellphone coverage at the time, and we were totally unable to communicate with each other. She was unaware of what was going on with us, and likewise, we were unaware of what was going on with them back in Ramadi.

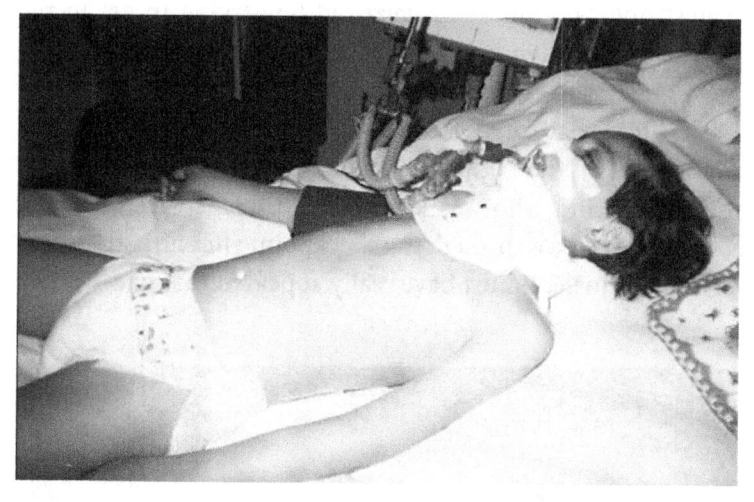

In the hospital in Baghdad, the day following the explosion.

My mother later told us she was unable to sleep from Wednesday to Sunday that week of the accident—"Not one hour." She was taking care of her boys. "It's a hard time. It's a very, very hard time," she told us. She also shared that my brother Ali had a dream, and he told her that everything was going to be OK.

Upon finally getting to the hospital in Baghdad, I was immediately taken to the intensive care unit. This was considered to be the best hospital in the country, so my father was at least consoled by that fact, even if only temporarily.

Our inability to communicate with my mother and brothers back in Ramadi during those first days in Baghdad added to our agony. Fortunately, after a few days, my mother and brothers were able to join us. Mohammed's and Ali's injuries were at the point where they could travel, so by the end of the week, the rest of the family had undertaken the same treacherous journey we had traveled to join us in Baghdad. We had family in Baghdad, and they provided the rest of our family with a place to stay, so for the next two months, that became our home. We were once again together as a family, but in a different city. I had yet to fully comprehend that neither I, nor my family, would ever again sleep in the home we had woken up in only a few days earlier. My health and my state of mind were still fragile. Physically, I was unable to speak or move. I had lost extensive amounts of blood. I was on a ventilator and given a tracheotomy, which was very uncomfortable, making it difficult to breathe and eat.

In the blink of an eye, our family's lifestyle had changed dramatically. The life we had known only days ago was no more. We were no longer in our home. My parents were no longer at their jobs as doctors. My brothers and I were no longer in school with our friends. I was in intensive care in a hospital I didn't know and unable to move. We had no home to return to and no future to point to. Our lives were no longer about my parents' careers and my brothers' and my schooling. It was beginning to center around one thing and one thing only . . . my care. The explosion that I continued to replay in my head had, in an instant, robbed us of everything we ever knew. My parents' careers no longer mattered. My brothers' lives no longer mattered. My father's vision for him and his family no longer mattered.

I was 8 years old and slowly coming to grips with the real possibility I would never walk again. Not only had the bombing ruined my life, but the lives of my entire family. My world, as I had known it, had come to an end, and I had taken my entire family down with me. At an age when I should be carefree and enjoying my childhood, I was beginning to sink into a deep, dark depression.

Throughout our stay in Baghdad, while I remained in intensive care in the hospital, my family was at my bedside every day. We were fortunate to have relatives in the area where my family members were able to stay during my hospitalization. All the while, my father was on the internet, making phone calls, using his connections in the medical community, doing anything and everything he could in his continued search for answers. What were the latest advancements in spinal cord injuries? Where were the best medical facilities? What sources of aid or assistance of any type were available? Were there trial procedures for someone in my situation, not yet proven, but in need of patients?

While I was dwelling on why this had happened and what would become of me, he was dwelling on finding answers. Whether it was his medical training, his personality, or both, he was singularly focused on the solution, as was the entire family. To me, I was in the abyss. To him, it was a challenge he was determined to find an answer to.

After I had spent nearly two months in intensive care, the doctors informed my parents they had done all they could do for me. If they had any hopes of my improving, they told them, they should look elsewhere. They had told my Dad that the Farrah Rehabilitation Center in Amman, Jordan, would be our next best option. That would mean not only leaving our home that we no longer had, but leaving the country.

In a period of fewer than sixty days, we had gone from the life we knew and enjoyed in Ramadi to a life without the use of my arms and legs, and with no home and no careers, to a hospital in Baghdad, and now, we were potentially heading to a foreign country and a very uncertain future. It was more than my 8-year-old mind could comprehend.

Throughout my fifty-five days in the hospital in Baghdad, my family had been extremely critical to my care and my basic survival. The nursing care was almost nonexistent because during and after the war, there were no regulations regarding who would take a position other than through connections. Most of the nurses there were not qualified and did not seem to care what happened to the patients. One nurse was telling my father how a patient died while he himself was sitting outside ignoring the alarms. Further, there were multiple occasions doctors told my parents to give up on my care because there was nothing else that could be done and that I would likely die.

If it were not for my family, I don't know if I would have survived.

Every night, my father slept on the floor next to my bed, getting only a few hours of sleep during the day, when others were available to help. While he slept, my brothers Mustafa and Mohammed would try to comfort me and keep me entertained by playing cartoons for me and remaining with me.

My mother spent virtually every waking hour in my room, caring for me, reading me stories, and trying to make me smile. Ali was still recovering from his own severe injuries, but I was able to see him on occasion.

My eldest uncle would come to visit often and would bring fresh honey, which he knew I loved. Other than the honey he would bring to encourage me to eat, most of my nutrition was through feeding tubes.

Those fifty-five days in Baghdad were the ultimate test of my family's devotion and determination to my survival. They, as much as the medical staff, were essential to my care. Those fifty-five days would also be the final days of our lives in our home country.

CHAPTER 4

Goodbye to Our Homeland

A MOVE TO JORDAN was not like going from Ramadi to Baghdad or Fallujah or any other city in Iraq. Our country was in the midst of war. The lives we had known just two months ago were destroyed by that war. My mobility was robbed from me by that war. And there were no more options available to us in the country that offered the health care my injuries required. Everything we were doing from this point forward was not a matter of preference ... it was a matter of survival!

We were leaving the country of our birth, and chances were strong that we would not be coming back. Iraq was our homeland. We had family in Iraq. This was not a move to be taken lightly. But it was a move we were forced to make. And it did not come without a flood of complications. My father was determined to address each of them. He diligently researched all options and reached out to any person or organization who could assist us with the complicated venture.

For starters, my health care costs would be staggering. In Iraq, health care is free. This was not the case in Jordan. We would need $20,000 to $30,000 in cash just to pay for the cost of the health care. This was at a time when my parents were no longer working. My father had accumulated savings and borrowed additional monies from our extended family, but that would not be an endless supply of income. In Jordan, where health care was very expensive, our cost of living would skyrocket at a time the family's resources were dwindling.

Then there was the matter of just getting into the country. Iraq was in the midst of war. Middle Eastern countries were being flooded with refugees, and many of the countries in the region, including Jordan, had placed severe restrictions on immigration. The border-crossing lines were extremely long, and people would often camp out just waiting to enter the country. There were even people who would make a living by driving people from Iraq to Jordan. The sheer volume of immigrants and refugees was overwhelming.

Getting in would be the first challenge. Staying in once we got there would be the next. The country had placed a six-month restriction on immigrants given what was becoming a growing refugee issue in the region. We would have to renew our visas every six months to justify a continued stay.

Knowing those issues awaited us, finally there were the complications of physically transporting me to another country in my condition. I was still in intensive care and totally without the use of my arms and legs. A commercial flight to Amman was only a one-hour flight. But given my situation, that one-hour flight would require special accommodations. The thought of flying in my condition was overwhelming to me . . . to another country, no less. But, given the situation in Iraq, I took some consolation in the fact we would be out of that danger zone.

Arrangements had to be made with the hospital in Jordan, and the airplane would have to be configured to accommodate my circumstances. My father was determined and took matters into his own hands. He made the arrangements with the hospital, secured the necessary medical supplies and equipment for the trip, and prepared a virtual intensive care facility on the plane for the one-hour flight.

With the final preparations and arrangements in place, on May 17, nearly two months after that fateful day, my father, my mother, and I left for Jordan, while my three brothers remained behind with extended family members to continue their schooling.

Once again, our family would be separated. Our first separation had occurred when my father transported me from Ramadi to Baghdad. Given the chaotic circumstances of that day and my inability to speak, that time apart was agonizing. This would be another one, borne from my circumstance.

The plane was a regular civilian plane, which my parents had to physically reconfigure to accommodate my medical condition. They transformed a row of seats into a makeshift hospital bed, complete with the ventilator and all other medical supplies. They took full responsibility for my transport without any aid from the Iraqi health department or the government.

Though Jordan was our neighboring country, there would be many obstacles to contend with. The government agencies were challenging for Iraqis. The heath care facilities were not particularly helpful. Plus, there were physical dangers.

During those days, despite enduring threats on his life, my father would go to every agency in the country to try to get me better care or to get me transported. He went to the Department of Health on two separate occasions seeking assistance. The first was to look for help from the Iraqi representatives, with no luck. And the second was to speak with the American representative. She asked my father if the Americans were the ones who injured him, and he stated that he did not know. The response was that they could not help, not even with transportation. Despite the distance and the physical risks, he went to a local branch of a Jordanian hospital to seek the care I would need.

When we arrived at the airport in Amman, just as my father had arranged, an ambulance was waiting to transport us to the Jordan Hospital. The primary focus at the facility was the surgeries to remove the shrapnel that was still in my body from the bombing, and these occurred a week after my arrival on May 25. Though the surgeons were unable to remove all of the shrapnel, I remained in the Jordan Hospital for five days before being transferred to the Farah Rehabilitation Institute, also in Amman, for additional treatments.

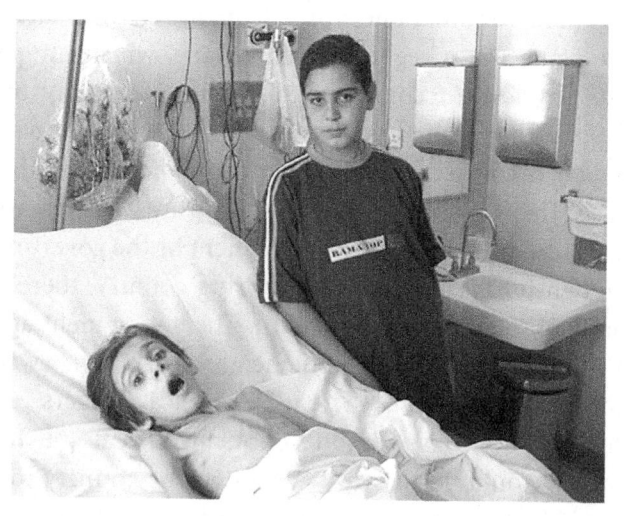

Not my best look. With my brother, Ali, in our early months
in Jordan, 2006.

There, after eighty-six days of not being able to breathe on my own, I was able to have the tracheotomy removed that become so much a part of my anatomy from the explosion. I was there for a period of four months, dealing with the myriad of health woes I was suffering from, including the added complications of bed sores and scoliosis.

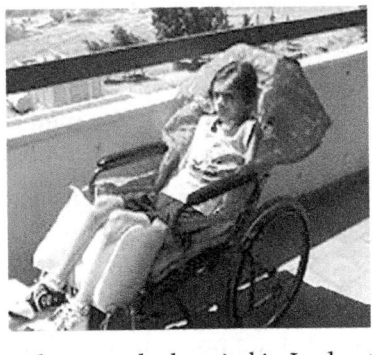

A rare visit outdoors, at the hospital in Jordan three months after the incident in 2006. Not a happy time.

In addition, I was falling into a deep depression. Despite having had the tracheotomy removed and now having the ability to eat, I was unwilling to eat. Though my parents and the hospital staff were begging me to eat, I would not start enjoying food again until I left the hospital.

By this time, my mother had returned to Iraq to finalize our affairs there and to retrieve my three brothers who were finishing their schooling. I missed my brothers terribly and looked forward to the time they and my mother would reunite with my father and me in Jordan.

The health care in Jordan, though very expensive, was an upgrade from the care I had received in Iraq. From the Jordan Hospital to the Farah Rehabilitation Center, the quality of the care was good, and the staff seemed to go out of their way to be helpful. It seems they developed a fondness for this little

8-year-old Iraqi who had become paralyzed. Given my physical condition and the emotional issues I was dealing with, I appreciated their kindness and their efforts to keep things light and upbeat.

The realities of what had happened to me were just beginning to sink in. My emotions ranged from being scared, to angry, to guilty. My entire family's lives had been turned upside down because of my condition. My father gave up his medical practice, my mom gave up her medical practice, and my brothers were no longer with their friends and were no longer able to focus on their own lives, but instead were forced to focus on mine.

Those first couple of months in Jordan were difficult for me, physically and emotionally. I felt the weight of the world was on my 8-year-old shoulders, when in reality, it was on the shoulders of my family.

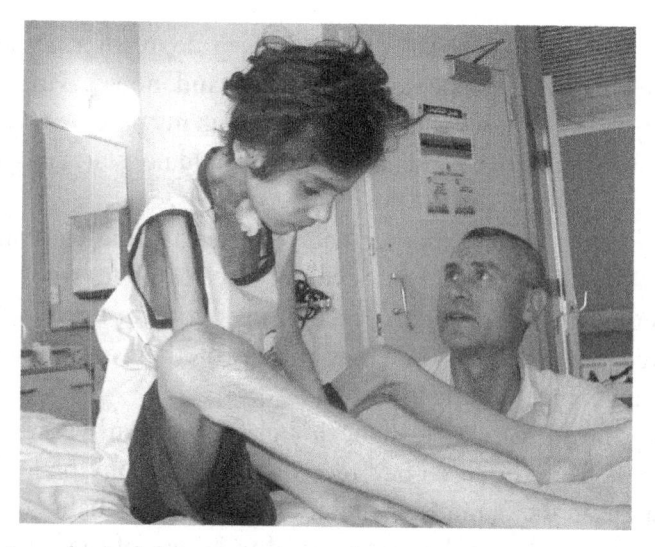

In a physical therapy session in the Jordanian hospital, with my physical therapist, Ahmed Bati in 2006.

When my mom and brothers finally joined my father and me in Jordan, I was very happy that we were once again a cohesive family unit. I looked up to my older brothers, and having them with me once again was a big emotional boost for me. With everyone once again together, but now in Jordan, it was a stark reminder that the home and the life we knew back in Ramadi were becoming a distant memory.

For me, the first few months in Jordan revolved around my health care from one hospital to the next. For my parents and brothers, those first few months were a matter of transition. Under the most ideal conditions, relocation can be challenging. Our conditions, however, were far from ideal. We were in a new city, a new country, with me overwhelming the family with medical expenses and my father with no job.

My family, first of all, had to find a new place to live. I say "my family" because I was still spending my time in the hospital. They secured an apartment that was within our restricted budget at the time, and that would accommodate the family, including the accommodations for me, once I was released from the hospital.

My father had secured a part-time position, leveraging his medical expertise by working in medical offices, but his income was a mere fraction of what he was earning as a physician in Iraq. After my accident, my mother had quit her job as an eye doctor to pretty much dedicate herself to my care. She, like my father, was consumed with my recovery, and she was now a full-time stay-at-home mom and caregiver.

Due to my father being our only source of income, combined with the fact that we had very costly medical expenses, our time in Jordan was one of living on a very tight budget.

They would have to enroll my brothers, and eventually me, into new schools. Education was a high priority in our family, and the disruption of a war was not going to get in its way. That also turned out to be a difficult transition.

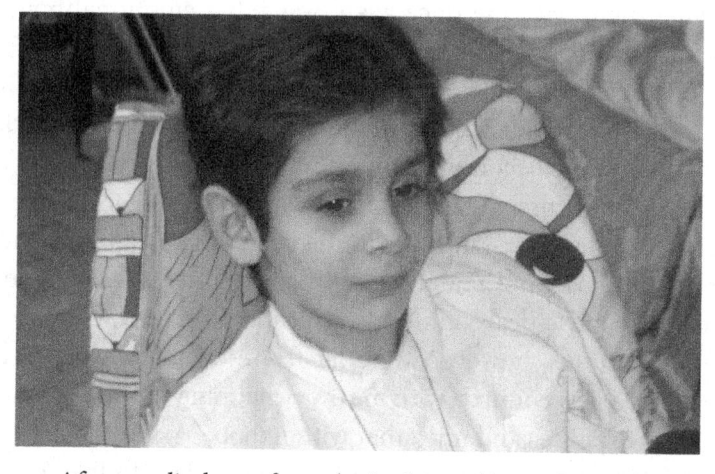

After my discharge from the Jordanian hospital in 2006.

Private schools were very expensive, and given our very tight family budget, they was out of the question. My brothers were enrolled and began attending public schools. Soon, they were in new schools, making new friends and getting immersed in their new coursework.

That was not an option for me.

There was a school for children with special needs, but only Jordanians were allowed to attend. Being an immigrant from Iraq, I was out of luck.

My father was not to be denied. He leveraged whatever contacts he could leverage, pulled whatever strings he could pull, and pleaded my case. Whatever he did, he was able to ultimately receive a waiver for me. But it required us to provide our own transportation back and forth, and we were without a car. So that was not an option.

The resulting solution was that once I was released from the hospital, I would be homeschooled, which would be another expense I was imposing on my family at a time when our finances were very tight. Meanwhile, I was still hospitalized at Farah Rehabilitation Center, where I was still receiving treatment and undergoing therapy in hopes of mitigating the severity of my paralysis. I enjoyed engaging with the staff, and they seemed to enjoy it as well. In fact, my brother Mohammed joked that by the time he and the others arrived from Iraq, I had already made friends with pretty much everyone at the Jordanian hospital. My mother remembers everyone at the rehab facility joking with me to make me smile.

That was my mechanism for dealing with my situation. I had shrapnel throughout my body. I was paralyzed from the neck down. I was developing scoliosis and bed sores. My ability to interact and make jokes with the family and hospital staff was my salvation.

During my time in the rehab center and following being bedbound, I was finally moved to a wheelchair for the first time in three months. I felt a new surge of energy and hope.

There was a time when my hair was growing longer, and there was constant commentary about my long hair and me looking like a girl. More than one well-wisher told my mom they would be praying for her daughter. At the time, getting a haircut was the last thing we were concerned about, but I'm glad to have provided my family a source of humor.

After months in the Farah facility, I was discharged and able to continue my treatment on an outpatient basis. For the first time in four months since that day, I was able to go home and be with my family. I graduated from a hospital bed to a wheelchair. I was still paralyzed from the neck down, and it was a manually operated wheelchair, which meant I had to be pushed everywhere I went. But I was finally home with my family, and I got my first taste of Jordan and Jordanians outside of those hospital walls.

Celebrating my discharge from the hospital at a restaurant in Amman in 2006. From left are Mohammed, my Dad, my Mother, me, Mustafa, and Ali.

Jordan, my family and I quickly discovered, was a different country than Iraq. They had a different economy. They had different social norms. And there was a certain perception that many Jordanians had of Iraqis. There was the notion that most Iraqis had money and lived a certain lifestyle. That may have been us back in Ramadi, but it was certainly not the case now. There was also a certain stigma about Iraqi refugees who were fleeing the war and consuming Jordanian social services.

Perhaps they were leery of people coming from a war-torn country for fear of the refugees using up their resources.

Perhaps they were worried that terrorists would be slipping across the borders, taking advantage of a volatile situation next door to bring about havoc in a neighboring country.

Perhaps there was some sort of underlying prejudice towards Iraqis that we didn't understand.

Whatever it was, I remember feeling a sense of being unwanted or that my family was some sort of drain on society.

That sensation, however, was very different where we were living. We were welcomed into the local community where we had rented an apartment in Amman. We enjoyed worshipping in the local mosque and developed close friendships there. And my brothers had developed new friendships in their school.

Like everything else regarding our new lives in Jordan, the fortune of having achieved some level of mobility since being in Ramadi also brought its challenges. I was in a wheelchair, but it was a manual wheelchair, which required family members to push me every place we went. The apartment we rented was on the second floor and there was no elevator, so my family needed to carry me with the chair on the stairs. Additionally, the hilly terrain of Amman did not make it easy for them. I would like to say that pushing me up and down the hills of Jordan provided my family good exercise. But they may describe it a very different way.

After my discharge from the hospital in Jordan in 2007. From left are Ali, my father, me, my Uncle Hashim, and Mustafa.

Enjoying the simple pleasures of being with my family and exploring this new country with them was exhilarating to me. But I was well aware of the burden it placed on them, and the continuing dangers in our homeland.

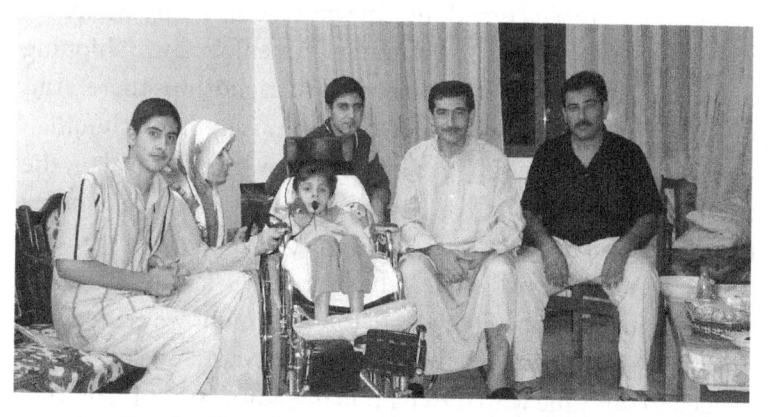

Another family gathering with my Uncle Hashim in 2006. From left are Mohammed, my mom, me, Mustafa, my dad, and Uncle Hashim.

It was during this time that we heard about our cousin going missing on his way home from the pharmacy back in Iraq. He's been missing since then. Even though we no longer lived there, we still had our family there and could not ignore what was happening to them every day.

CHAPTER 5

A Brief Side Trip to Russia

W HEN YOU'RE A parent and you have a child who needs your help, there is virtually nothing you wouldn't do to find that help. There is no stone you would not turn, no experiment you would not try, no risk you would not take. At least, that was my father's attitude.

Throughout our time since the bombing, from Ramadi, to Baghdad, and now in Jordan, my father was constantly scouring the Web and inquiring throughout the medical community, looking for potential medical breakthroughs or innovative therapies that could address my paralysis.

While in Jordan, my parents learned of a stem-cell procedure that was being performed on spinal cord injury patients that might help my situation. My father began doing some investigation around stem-cell procedures, which, despite their somewhat controversial nature in the United States, were being performed in other countries around the world.

China and Russia were two of those countries.

At first, my father reached out to China to learn more about the procedure and to see if we qualified, but we were denied a visa. I don't know if the Chinese government was wary of

Iraqi immigrants, given the state of the war in our country, or if they just had strict immigration policies that applied to every country. Whichever it was, that door was closed to us. That did not deter my father, however. It was on to the next option.

He began exploring the Russian option. He established email correspondence with various Russian officials and medical professionals. The more he was told, the more he became hopeful about the possibilities.

You obviously treat anything new with a degree of skepticism, especially when it is from a foreign country and involves significant logistics and expenses. My father applied the necessary due diligence to the situation, especially from the vantage point of being a medical professional.

He was also a father who was determined to find a solution for his quadriplegic son, and the messages he was receiving were promising. One Russian physician even boldly stated to my father, "We are going to get your son walking again, back on his legs!"

The prospect of me once again being able to walk was exciting, but we took the news with what I would describe as *a skeptical hopefulness.*

Hope is a good thing, and something we as a family desperately needed, but my father was trained not to get overly excited about something that may or may not happen.

Being as young as I was, and as recent as the bombing had been, I was still coming to grips with the reality of my situation. From fear, to anger, to self-pity, to depression, my emotions were all over the place at that time, and it was difficult for me to be hopeful about anything!

My mother and father, however, saw things differently. With their training, their experience, their wisdom, and being parents, if there was any possibility to see me walk again, and to see our family get our lives back, they had no choice but to move. That was the sole reason we were in a foreign country, risking everything and spending thousands of dollars . . . to get help for me and regain our sense of purpose as a family.

They could not afford *not* to pursue the possibility. The decision was made.

If the ambulance ride from Ramadi was agonizing, and the plane ride from Baghdad to Jordan was scary and fraught with issues, the notion of going to Russia was downright terrifying. I was still a young kid, without the use of my body. My entire sense of safety and security centered around the stability of having a consistent routine and being surrounded by the love and support of my family. Going to Russia did not offer that stability. It was a four-and-a-half-hour flight to a country that was cold and depressing, where no one spoke our language.

Jordan was not our home country. But at least it was in the Middle East, where the weather was warm and the people spoke our language. Russia was none of that. I should have been excited about the possibility of being able to walk again. Instead, I was sad. I was depressed and going to a depressing place. And, once again, I would be leaving my mother and my brothers.

I had a very difficult time saying goodbye to my mother and my brothers. I had always been very family oriented, but given the events of the past year, I had become even more so. Boarding that plane to go to Russia, especially when everything regarding the procedure was so uncertain, was a difficult thing to do. But we had to find out.

When my father and I arrived in Moscow, the challenges began almost immediately, while we were still at the airport, and these were a foreshadowing of the difficulties that lay ahead.

We had to enlist the services of an interpreter while in Russia because of the language barrier. Being a doctor, my father did speak some English, but unfortunately, he spoke no Russian, so we needed some help if we were going to converse with the doctors and hospital staff in Moscow.

We were strangers in a strange land in search of a procedure we were not sure existed. My emotions veered from being anxious to being outright frightened. I had developed a fondness for the treatment of the hospital staff in Jordan and had no indication that I would be greeted the same way here.

I was already grappling with depression from the events of the past year and my condition. During our brief stay in Russia, my depression worsened. Once I was in the hospital, my father was busy in meetings regarding my potential treatment. I was left in my hospital room with an attendant during his meetings. I was an 8-year-old boy in a foreign land staying in a strange room with a complete stranger.

There was one meeting that lasted longer than expected. I was in my room, alone with a nurse, growing increasingly anxious and agitated as the meeting continued. As each minute passed, my imagination took over and it led me to think I was being abandoned. My imagination took over. I became convinced I was being abandoned. I had concluded that I had become too much of a burden to my family, and that my father had left me there all alone.

They had been forced to give up their entire existence because of my condition, I had rationalized, and had decided it had become too much for the family to bear.

As absurd as that sounds today, that was the state of my 8-year-old mind during those days in Russia. Depression, guilt, anxiety, and fear were constant emotions for me during that time. And now, the fear of abandonment had crept into my head. I was probably in the worst place emotionally that I had been in since the bombing, and I was never so happy to see my father walk back into my room after his meeting.

In the final analysis, the trip turned out to be a bitter disappointment. We left after three days.

After many conversations and sending detailed records and over eight thousand dollars in cash to the Russian officials in advance, we learned the trip would be for naught. In his meetings, my father discovered that the procedure was still in somewhat of a research phase, and that my spinal cord injury was just too advanced to benefit from the operation. He also learned that while the physicians had performed the procedure on adults, they had no experience in performing the procedure on children.

Essentially, we had spent three days and upwards of $10,000 to learn something we could have learned from Jordan, had the Russians been more honest and up front. My father had done everything they had requested in advance of the trip, including sending my detailed medical records. There was no question that the medical team didn't know, though they certainly should have known in advance, what they were dealing with.

Could the communications have been that bad? Or, had we been duped? Was the entire proposition a scam?

We were returning to Jordan from an expensive venture with nothing to show for it. At a time when neither of my parents were working and friends and family had chipped in to help us finance the venture, we had no good news to share with them.

My father was frustrated and even angry, and I was still dealing with my depression and guilt. I was, however, after spending three days in a hospital room in a cold, depressing country, returning to our home in Jordan to see my mother and my brothers.

Amman, Jordan, had never looked so good.

For me, the Russia trip was a very distressing one. I remember thinking, "What kind of a low-life person or group of people would take advantage of refugees who were forced to flee their war-torn home and whose son was catastrophically injured during a wartime bombing? Who would be disgusting enough to take advantage of a family whose youngest boy wants nothing but to walk again?"

For my father, however, beyond his initial disappointment and frustration, he had a very different attitude. I'm reminded of the famed inventor Thomas Edison, who said, "Every failure gets me closer to a solution."

My father had the same mindset. If the remedy for my son's condition doesn't reside in Russia, he reasoned, it must reside elsewhere.

Upon our return to Jordan, he resumed his quest, both for me and for our family.

CHAPTER 6

Back to Jordan

W E RESUMED OUR lives in Jordan. We were a family again. We were living in a cramped apartment. My father was working part time for a medical supply office. My mother was working at home as a full-time health care provider for me. My brothers were attending the local schools. I was being homeschooled.

My parents and my brothers had established friends, both in their schools and at the mosque. The war that was taking place in Iraq was still ongoing and forever in our thoughts. But we were in a safer situation.

We engaged in activities in the area and made trips into the city. We were without a car, and this required us to walk, and I was in a wheelchair that required my family members to push me everywhere we went. The hilly terrain made that a difficult task. I was dependent on my brothers and my parents for virtually everything, from routine movements, to eating, to going to the bathroom.

Our time in Jordan was extremely difficult. We were on a very tight budget. Getting the four of us the continued education that was so important to my parents was challenging.

And all the while, my father was in search of care for me and a new life for our family, and he wasn't sure there would be a light at the end of this long dark tunnel we were in. Given how bad things had become in Iraq, Jordan did provide us a place to move, even though there were challenges.

There were some bright spots, however.

Over the period of two years, we developed several new friendships in Jordan, through attending religious services at the local mosque. I spent a lot of my time watching television, reading books and playing outdoors with some of my new friends I made.

This photograph of me was taken by my friend, Mohammed, in 2007. Mohammed later died of cancer.

Though limited in what they were able to do for my care, the health care was a step up from the care we had received in Iraq, but very expensive. The health care workers were professional and friendly and seemed genuinely concerned for my situation. The surgeries to remove the shrapnel from my body and to remove the tracheotomy I had been living with were also a blessing.

But Jordan was not our home, nor did we believe it would be.

Given what was going on in our country, Jordan offered us a temporary safe haven from the war, but we had become convinced it would not be a long-term solution for us. We decided that if we were going to get the quality of medical care I would need and anything close to the quality of life we had once enjoyed, we would have to look elsewhere.

Through it all, my father continued his search for a solution to our situation and mine.

There were thoughts about going to Syria. It is our next-door neighbor. It is part of the Middle East. It shares our cultural and religious roots; plus, it is a beautiful country. However, Syria was also beginning to experience the same kind of political volatility and upheaval we had just left. In hindsight, given the many problems that followed in that country, we are fortunate to have decided against moving there.

The more my father searched and the more he learned, it appeared that the answers lay somewhere in the Western countries.

We considered a wide range of options with a number of factors to be considered. There was the issue of the health care I would need for my recovery. There was also the issue of potential job opportunities for my parents, as well as the issue of educational opportunities that would be available to my brothers and me. And, all of that would have to be factored into the basic living expenses we would incur and the quality of living we could achieve.

Then there was the issue of politics, prejudices, and the overall receptiveness we would receive as Iraqis. Saddam

Hussein and the war in our country were still very polarizing factors throughout the world, in some places more than others.

We thought about Europe . . . possibly Germany or the U.K. The quality of life, health care, and education had their appeal, but we weren't sure about the cultural fit or the job opportunities that would be available to my parents. So, ultimately, we decided against that option as well.

And then, there was the U.S.

On its surface, going to the very country that had destroyed the lives we had once enjoyed in Iraq, not to mention my mobility, seemed far-fetched. This was the country that had destroyed our home and our way of living. It was a country that had strong anti-Arab sentiments. This was the country that had destroyed all that was sacred in our home country. This was the country that sent soldiers into our neighborhoods, kicking down doors and arresting family members.

America, as we knew it, was a paradox for us . . . it offered the highest quality of living we could hope to achieve, yet it was the evil empire that robbed us of all we had ever owned.

On the other hand, America seemed to have the health care I would need. It obviously offered the quality of life we sought. It represented the educational opportunities that my parents wanted for my brothers and me. And, it represented the possibility of my parents being able to resurrect their medical practices.

There was no question that the country could potentially offer us the qualities of life we would hope to regain. But the United States? Going to the United States, in my mind, was like going to live with the den of lions that had eaten a family member. The sheer thought of it frightened me.

But in the same spirit my father had maintained since the beginning of our vagabond existence, his attitude and conviction remained constant ... leave no stone unturned. Consider every possibility. Reject no potential option.

Should we take this seemingly unimaginable step? No. Should we consider it and explore the possibilities? Absolutely!

The United States was now on our radar as our possible solution.

CHAPTER 7

Considering America

WE HAD A lot of assumptions about America, some good, some bad. But, for the most part, the country was a big unknown. Geographically, America was on the other side of the world. Culturally, however, it may as well have been on a completely different planet. The language, the culture, the biases, the political climate—all of those issues were big question marks for us.

For me, the most predominant feeling I had at the thought of moving to the United States was fear. By that time, I was nine years old, and I still remembered the anxiety I'd felt just moving from one house to another. Moving to an entirely different part of the world, especially the United States, felt overwhelming.

My only frame of reference of Americans were the U.S. soldiers during wartime. They were big, hulking, faceless men. Everything about them provoked fear and anxiety. Were all Americans like that? Were they bad people? Would they be receptive to us? Did they hate Iraqis?

I constantly worried about how we would be received and

treated in the United States, especially given how we were initially treated by the Jordanians when we first moved to that country. The unknowns were endless and a little much for my young mind to take in.

My family later told me that out of all of us, I was the one who most resisted moving to the U.S. Yet, at the same time, my religious upbringing reassured me that everything happens for a reason, and if my family said moving to America was the best thing we could do, I guess I was on board.

Let's Try It Out . . .

Eventually, we decided to test the waters.

In 2007, my parents engaged an international refugee organization who connected them with an Egyptian family living in Royersford, Pennsylvania. They decided my mother and I, just the two of us, would take the plunge to scope out the place before the entire family would relocate halfway around the world.

According to the arrangements, we would stay with the family for a month.

After solidifying our plans with the agency and the family, we began learning everything we could about the pending trip. First of all, where was Royersford, Pennsylvania, and what did we know about this family we would be sharing a home with for a month in a foreign land?

We began studying U.S. geography and learned that Royersford is a small town of about 5,000 people, located in the state of Pennsylvania on a river we could not pronounce and about an hour outside of Philadelphia. Later, after I had learned to read and write in English, I discovered that the spelling of the name of the river and the pronunciation of that name were totally different. It is spelled the "Schuylkill" River, but the locals pronounce it "skoolkill." Our family would later learn that happens a lot in the English language. We learned that while originally from Egypt, the family had been living in America for many years. They seemed to have a good grasp on the country and its culture, and spoke English very well. They had a very positive view of the country, and from all we could learn, my parents were convinced the family would serve as safe and reliable guide for my mother and me in our first venture to America.

Now, all I had to do was prepare myself, emotionally and physically, for this adventure I was about to undertake, which included psyching myself up for the twelve-hour plane ride. I learned from my previous travels that I am not a great traveler, even under the best of circumstances. I suffered bouts of car sickness when I was younger, even on a two-hour drive. Now, I would have to travel by plane for *twelve* hours . . . to a strange country full of unknowns . . . where people spoke a language I didn't understand . . . knowing no one . . . while being confined to a wheelchair . . . without my father and brothers to look after me! I agonized over the very thought of the trip and can remember crying myself to sleep on more than one occasion leading up to our planned departure.

The only thing I would have was the protective guidance of my mother and the faith I had been taught that this, too, was happening for a reason.

Thankfully, with those reassurances, as the time grew closer, I was able to summon the courage to take on the adventure head-on. I had been convinced and now believed this trip would be the beginning of a better life for all of us. And though I was the youngest and the least physically equipped, my mother and I would be blazing a trail for the rest of our family. I had no choice but to be strong.

It was summertime of 2007 when we arrived in Pennsylvania. The weather was warm, and everything around us was an adventure. The climate reminded me of the warmth of our homeland and stood in contrast to the bitter cold we experienced during our time in Russia.

After landing in Philadelphia, we were transported out to the town of Royersford, about an hour away. Though the landscape was lush with trees, hills, and rivers, it all seemed to be just a continuous extension of the city of Philadelphia.

The family that would be our hosts for the next month consisted of a middle-aged couple with three sons and a daughter. Nice as they were, the living situation became the next of the many surprises and discoveries on our journey.

My mother was taken aback when she learned upon our arrival that the family consisted of a husband and three sons. In other cultures, that may not be unusual, but in our religion, women are not supposed to be living around men, much less in the same house with men who are not related to them without having her own husband with her.

Needless to say, my mother was surprised and a bit frustrated to learn of the proposed living arrangement, especially since she was led to believe that we would only be staying with a mother and daughter. This would be the first of many instances where we experienced the challenges of communicating across different languages, cultures, and countries. Somewhere between those channels, the communication was lost while making the arrangements through the relocation organization.

My mother's first reaction was to immediately cancel our trip and return home, which would have been fine with me. I was already missing my father and brothers. But after speaking with my father by phone, she was convinced to stay. Having come this far, they concluded, to turn around at this juncture would be very, very unwise. We came here for a reason, they agreed, and we could not let something like a little mix-up cause our trip to be wasted.

Having decided to stay, we settled in and found our hosts to be extremely nice and hospitable. They arranged living quarters for us in the basement, which was a comfortable living space, and this made it easier for my mother because of the cultural and religious norms.

Our trip to the U.S. was an adjustment for the entire family. We were learning a lot with our new family in this foreign land and were very actively involved in the issue of my health care. But we were sorely missing my father and brothers. As it turns out, they were missing us just as much. My brother Mohammed joked that he was forced to learn to cook during our time away, since my mother, the resident chef in our home, was far, far away from the family stove.

Eventually, we even decided to extend our stay. In addition to our time in Royersford, my mother and I also spent some time at a Ronald McDonald House in nearby Camden, New Jersey.

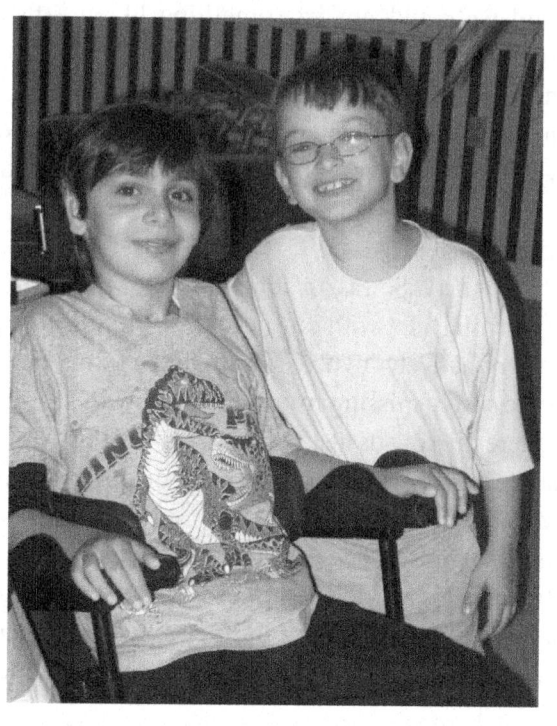

At the Ronald McDonald House in New Jersey during my first
visit to the U.S. with my mother in 2007. This is one of my
first American friends, Cody.

Geographically, Camden, close to Royersford, is in the state
of New Jersey. Camden and Philadelphia are like sister cities,
only separated by that river whose name I could not pronounce.

The facility we were staying in was pretty nice, but the location
left a lot to be desired. The city was filled with littered streets,
burned-out and abandoned buildings, and rough-looking
tenement houses. We later learned that Camden is consistently
named one of the most dangerous cities in America. That was
one of the many ironies of our visit. We came from a war-

ravaged country, only to be in an area of the U.S. that appeared to be just as rough.

In parallel with the many surprises and discoveries of our trip, there were definitely some highlights to match. One of them was that I was learning the English language. Through conversations with the Egyptian family we were staying with, who spoke the language very well, as well as through watching American cartoons and having my mom read to me, I began to develop a good grasp of the language. People would later tell me how impressed they were to learn that I learned an entirely new language in such a short amount of time.

Another highlight was that I received a power wheelchair for the first time. Getting around in a manual chair is quite difficult, especially when you're a young boy. It was hard on myself as well as my family members, who would take turns pushing me around. In addition to the normal limitations of being wheelchair bound, I felt bad that my family members were regularly given the task of pushing me wherever we went.

Getting a motorized wheelchair was the equivalent of a teenager getting their first car or going from horse and buggy to motorized vehicles. My mom and I were absolutely thrilled when I got the motorized chair, as my father and my brothers would be when we returned home.

Which brings me to the second major purpose of our visit to the U.S. In addition to assessing whether or not we might want to move to America as a permanent move, my parents also wanted me to take advantage of the health care facilities in the country. So, while there, in addition to learning about the many nuances of American life, much of my time was spent undergoing physical therapy, and I was transported by a van provided by the Shriners' charitable organization to and from a nearby hospital for my scheduled treatments.

All in all, our initial trip to America was a good one. We found the people friendly and far more accepting of us than I had first thought they would be. The health care facilities were nice, as was the overall state-of-the-art health care in terms of advancements, medicines, treatments, and health care professionals.

My mother and I both felt a lot more positive about the country after having stayed here for a few months, as we did about the people . . . people we would someday call friends, neighbors, classmates, and colleagues.

My father greeting my mom and me upon our return from our visit to America in 2007. The man on the left was instrumental in helping us with our visit.

Keep in mind, our only exposure to Americans prior to our visit had been the American soldiers who would bust into our homes unannounced in the middle of the night holding guns to our heads and ransacking our home. To discover people who were warm and friendly and cared about our plight was a heartwarming surprise to my mom and me. We even found Americans who were not supportive of their government's invasion into Iraq and were sympathetic to our circumstance.

This was a dramatic departure from the assumptions we had about the country and its people before our visit.

My mom and I both were prepared to return home and recommend to my father and brothers that this should be our new home. Imagine that . . . all the pain and disruption we had experienced because of the United States, and now it was the very country we wanted to call home.

I am happy to say that our impression of the United States changed for the better after my mother and I took our trip.

The trip was, in fact, so successful that when we went back to Jordan and told everyone about what we did and what we had learned, the decision was made to move to the U.S. for good.

CHAPTER 8

The Decision

FROM THOSE VERY first days after the bombing, my father began a nonstop quest to find the treatment I would need, and at the same time, to re-establish a home for our family. There was no internet site regarding spinal injuries that he had not searched. And there was seemingly no medical professional he had not consulted. It is that quest that took us from our home in Ramadi, to Baghdad, to Jordan, and even to Russia.

And everywhere we went, he continued to hear the same answer . . . if you want the best treatment options for your son, and the best place to rebuild your life, you must go to America. From medical professionals around the globe and organizations, including Amnesty International, the message was the same . . . our only option was to go to America as refugees.

That would not only be a huge change for us in terms of my parents getting jobs and us settling into a new land and a different culture, but we were living in a time when our two countries were at war. America was the enemy. America was the country that had destroyed our home . . . and my mobility.

We were Iraqi and we were Muslims. And those were perhaps the least popular species in America at the time. We had to prepare ourselves for the possibility of a steady dose of discrimination.

The only real situations we had previously experienced with Americans prior to my mom and I visiting the country were with the American soldiers in Iraq, and that was a mixture of good and bad. From kicking in our front door in search of militia, to the many military roadblocks we experienced during the ambulance ride to Baghdad, American soldiers had not created a positive impression for my parents. There were exceptions, but those were few and far between.

When my mom and I returned to rejoin our family in Jordan with positive feedback about the country we had once scorned, the decision was made.

Shortly after our move to the U.S. in 2008. From left are Mustafa, our Dad, me, Ali, and Mohammed.

The country that was responsible for the destruction of our old home in Ramadi would now become our new home. With the assistance of Amnesty International and the Shriners Hospital, we made plans to leave Jordan and the Middle East and become Americans. We would move to the birthplace of the country's independence, Philadelphia, Pennsylvania.

Transitioning to a new city is complicated, even under the best of circumstances. Transferring from across the globe from a foreign country under refugee conditions brings with it yet another level of complications. We had an agency assisting us with the transition, but that, too, created even more complications.

Despite the many complications and frustrations we encountered from the transition, our life in the U.S. began in the small town of Villanova, Pennsylvania, a suburb of Philadelphia. Our first residence was not an apartment, but a dorm in the local mosque, which brought its own set of challenges. We were now in a housing arrangement with two small bedrooms and a half bathroom. Initially, I did not have easy wheelchair access, and, not having a car, my parents and older brothers had to rely on mass transit to get to job interviews, grocery stores, or pretty much anywhere, for that matter.

Eventually, we moved into a small, cramped apartment in another Philadelphia suburb called King of Prussia, where the challenges of becoming Americans continued.

My father, who was a physician back in Iraq, was not licensed to practice medicine in the United States. To become licensed, he would have to get additional schooling and take tests to be certified, and all of that would take time and money. And given the amount of money we had already spent on my health care, those things would have to wait. He had a more immediate objective, which was to support his family.

That required filling out job application after job application to do anything in the medical field he could do in the U.S. It seemed like a never-ending process that had to have been frustrating for a man who was a respected, licensed physician with a specialty as an allergist back in his country.

Thankfully, he secured a position as a volunteer working for a local allergist, and this provided him an introduction to the network of local medical professionals, allowing him to meet others in his field.

Those initial weeks and months living in the U.S. were difficult. As my brother Mohammed recalled, "We had to fight for everything. It was sort of figure-it-out-as-you-go."

And that's exactly what we did. We were figuring out how to become Americans.

I remember my father working extremely long hours to make ends meet. There was about a three-year period where he worked both a full-time and a part-time job, often leaving the house at six in the morning and not returning until around midnight. My brothers Mohammed and Mustafa worked part-time as well, leaving my mother to care for me on a full-time basis. I remember there being times when they had to work on the weekends.

Unfortunately, this was just the way things were in my family. One thing's for certain; everybody was pretty much occupied during that time in our lives.

For my parents, they had to worry about the basics of where to work, where to live, and how to get assimilated into our new country. For my brothers and me, a large part of figuring out how to become Americans was getting into the school system.

I was too young and largely immune to everything my parents had to go through just to get us into the country, much less get us settled into our new home. The biggest issue for me was getting into a new school and being confronted with American classmates. Transitioning from being homeschooled, which is how I learned while in Jordan, to attending public school upon our move to the United States was going to be a major transition.

How would I respond to the coursework? How would I be greeted by my fellow classmates . . . as an Iraqi . . . as a Muslim . . . being in a wheelchair? Those were questions that I was confronted with.

How would they treat me, being an Iraqi, much less being a disabled Iraqi? I was excited, but at the same time, fearful. I had all these apprehensions about facing an anti-Iraqi sentiment, an anti-Muslim sentiment, and the added distinction of being in a wheelchair.

I was just a little kid, and one who was new to this country and this culture. Plain and simple, I was scared. I had no idea what to expect. Would I make friends? Would I have trouble with my schoolwork? Would I be able to make it through the days on my own?

Up to that time, I was used to the constant help of family members to help me do, well, pretty much everything. My parents actually accompanied me during that first day of school back in 2008. When the principal asked my mom why she wasn't leaving, she simply told him, "Because he is my son." She said she would never forget those words. "I can't imagine my son going any place without me," my mother said.

Being that she had cared for me on a minute-by-minute basis since the moment I became injured, it was understandable that she would have trouble leaving my side. It actually ended up being that I was more scared on the second day of school, because I no longer had my parents right there with me.

I was thinking that my parents would be with me every day, like that first day, next to me to guide me through things and help me when I needed help. I was even more afraid and upset when they were no longer there.

I'm happy to say that I made it through that second day, and from there, things seemed to get much easier.

My fear and uncertainty had to do not only with the schoolwork. It was also the idea of socializing with others my age and making friends. It's hard when you move to a new school and don't know anybody. It's that much harder when you come from a different country in an entirely different part of the world. Transitioning from being homeschooled to attending public school in a different country, especially the United States, was a daunting experience. But, it was the beginning of a new life for me.

In 2009, I was in the seventh grade. I'm shown here giving a presentation of my experiences to a fifth-grade class. I was learning early that my life could have purpose.

All the other kids and teachers were really nice to me. People would talk to me and ask me about my life. They wanted to know things about my family and me. They seemed genuinely interested in me, which was a pretty great feeling.

And nobody seemed to treat me differently because of my paralysis. In fact, people went out of their way to help me get around school, doing things like helping me onto the elevator and such. I developed some good friends in those first months and years in middle school, and even more as I transitioned into high school.

As far as the coursework in the American schools, I progressed fairly well. My biggest challenges centered around math, but I felt comfortable with much of the other subject matter. My mother recalls that I would often insist on doing my homework entirely by myself with no assistance. I think I felt as though this was the only way I would learn.

The technology built into that chair coupled with laptop computers that were provided through our school district made learning and participating in class that much easier.

Because of my physical limitations, it took me much longer to do my schoolwork than it likely would take other children, and I remember there were days when I would not finish my homework until around ten or eleven o'clock at night.

Though I was becoming fairly proficient at navigating my schoolwork and the other aspects of living my life in a wheelchair, there was a time in 2013 when I would find myself back in the hospital. During my constant physical exams and checkups, it was determined that I was developing scoliosis in my spine. Though it was in its early stages, it was concluded that I should undergo surgery to correct it before it worsened.

Hospitalizations were nothing new to me; I had spent the greater portion of my life in and out of hospitals. But I was hoping that had become a thing of the past. The good news was that undergoing surgery to correct scoliosis, I told myself, would be a cakewalk compared to what I had previously endured.

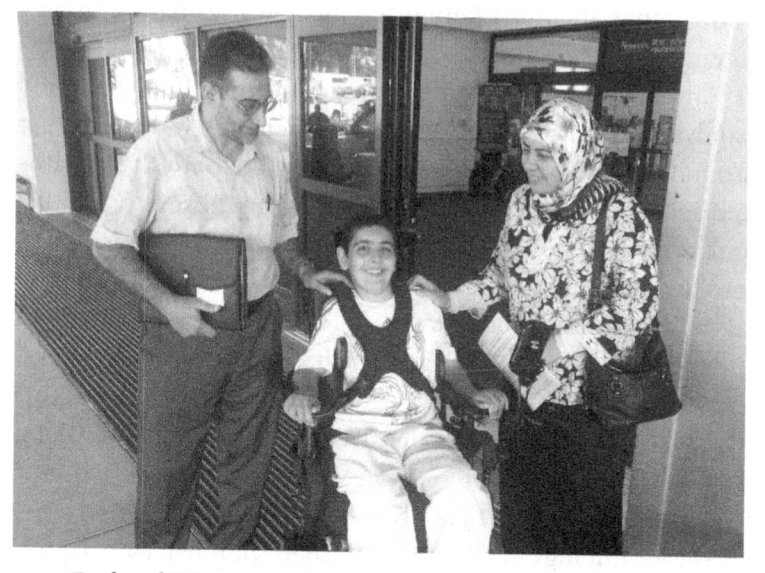

Dad and Mom encouraging me before my spinal surgery,
July 26, 2013.

In a small but significant way, this hospitalization was different. I was not there as a quadriplegic, hanging on to dear life. I was simply a patient having a routine surgical procedure, just like millions of others have surgical procedures. And I was being given the absolute best of care. Unlike so many in this world who don't have access to this level of care, I was indeed fortunate. Instead of dwelling on all that my family and I had been through since that day back in our home in Ramadi, I was now living in one of the most advanced countries on Earth, receiving excellent medical care and being loved and supported by an extraordinary family.

Yes, I was having back surgery. And, as the saying goes, there is no such thing as minor surgery. But overall, our lives were indeed getting better.

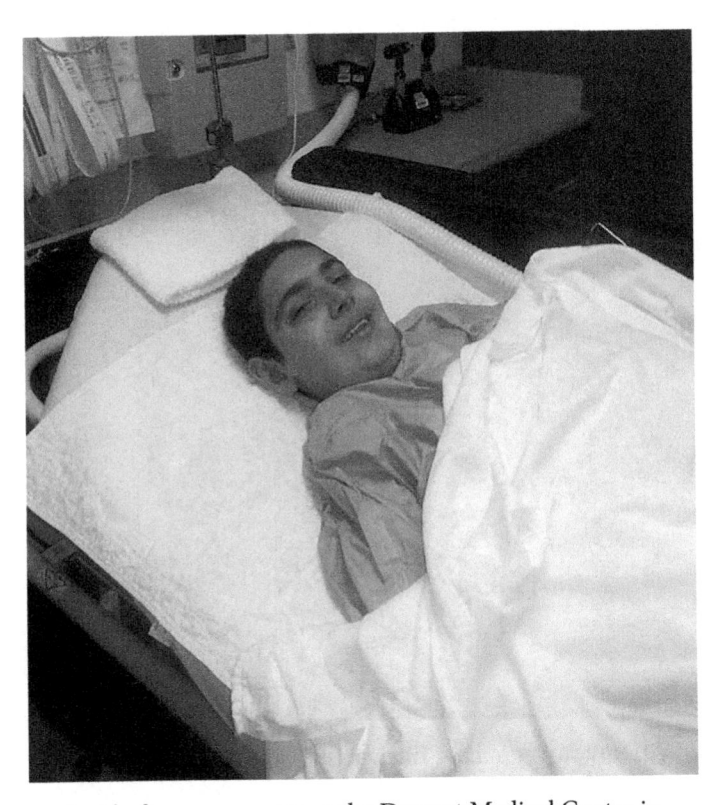

Just before my surgery at the Dupont Medical Center in
Delaware. The look of total confidence, right?

There were many growing pains in those early days in
America, but all in all, we got through the many start-ups and
transitions and began to learn the ins and outs of becoming
Americans. By high school, I felt as though I had a system
down, and I was able to both get through my schoolwork and
have a social life.

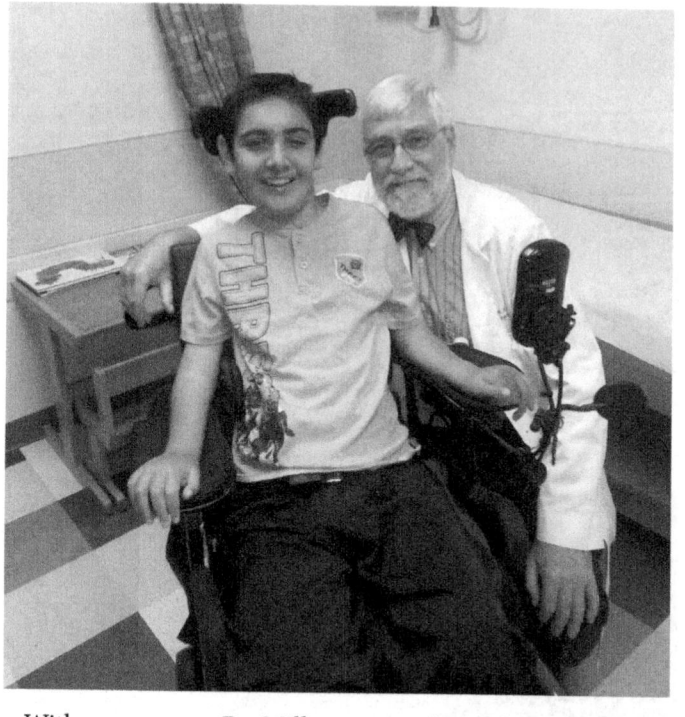

With my surgeon, Dr. Miller, at one of my follow-up visits.

All in all, I have fond memories of those first few days and weeks in school. For my brothers, however, it was a slightly different situation. My oldest brother, Mohammed, was 18 that year, and he recalls how difficult it was to transition into academia in a foreign land.

He had finished high school while we were still living in Jordan and had already gotten accepted to college in that country, but his plans would have to change when we decided to move to America. He eventually transitioned into a local community college, and my brothers Mustafa and Ali were still in high school. All three eventually went on to higher education, which was another issue of transition for us. In Iraq, college is free, but here in the U.S., it costs money, and lots of it.

That was yet another reason my father had to constantly be at work.

Looking back, those early concerns and fears I had about attending school in the U.S. were for naught. Overall, my new school was a very positive experience. I had no use of my arms, hand, legs, or feet. But I did have three things I could rely on: my ability to make friends, my brain, and the technology that was made available to me.

Those things, combined with our faith and the support of my parents and brothers, made the difference for me.

That was true for all of us. Our plans were now changed. Our focus was now learning a new language, in a new school and with new friends. Just as in every other aspect of our new life, we were figuring it out as we went along. We were now Americans, living in a country that was at war with our home country, learning its customs, its values, and its people. We had each other, and other than the random crime that takes place anywhere, we were safe. Safe to create a new home for ourselves.

CHAPTER 9

My Life, My Choice

FROM THE DAY the bombing occurred, I was thrust into a series of physical battles I would have never imagined. I had lost the use of my arms and legs and was completely dependent on my family and health care professionals for my every move. From eating a meal, to changing clothes, to going to the bathroom, I was a virtual invalid in every sense of the word.

For more than a dozen years now, since that March morning in 2006, I've been trapped inside a body that refuses to cooperate. My mind keeps sending signals to my body, but my body is not receiving them. They're not reaching their intended destination due to a severed spine, courtesy of a piece of shrapnel from the blast. My mind, thankfully, was totally unimpacted.

An active mind and an unresponsive body, however, make for an interesting combination. They are like a river that is dammed up and the water can no longer flow. The river keeps sending water, which has to go somewhere. It either creates new rivers or it floods the surrounding area. If my thoughts can't go one place, they go another.

There are countless stories of people who lose one bodily function and the brain compensates by highly developing other functions—like the singer Ray Charles, who was blind but developed a heightened sense of hearing, or Helen Keller, who was born both deaf and blind, but became a prolific author and spokeswoman for human rights.

Since that day, my mind has been overrun, both mentally and emotionally.

In those early days, there was no other way for me to look at my situation without concluding that my life was over. What more was there to live for, I would ask myself? I would no longer be able to run, to play with my brothers, to play sports, to feed myself, or even to take a bath. Given my age at the time, my view of life could not see beyond the narrow horizons of an 8-year-old. My world was filled with dark images of hopelessness and despair.

My parents and my brothers were constantly encouraging me and telling me we would find our way out of the dark place we occupied. Plus, my father was relentless in his determination to find a medical cure for my situation. But at night, when I was all alone, the fears, the questions, and the demons of hopelessness found their way into my thoughts.

How could I possibly function without the use of my body? What possible use could I be? I was nothing but a burden to my family. Their lives had been totally ruined because of me. In a matter of a flash, I had gone from being an active child and playing sports with my brothers to becoming a mere vegetable. The dreams of my parents and my brothers, I thought, were all shattered because of me. I was consumed by feelings of fear, guilt, uselessness, and depression. I saw no way out.

Those feelings weighed heavily on the mind of an 8-year-old, and they remained close at hand, even as my journey progressed. I just couldn't bring myself to accept the fact that I could no longer do the things I once did. It was painful for me to see other children doing things like playing soccer. I would often start crying just thinking about the things I loved doing but could no longer do.

As my family scurried around getting us settled in and acclimated from one location to the next, all I could do was lie in my bed, helplessly watching . . . all because of me. Those were the darkest, most depressing times of my life.

As the years progressed, I watched as my father maintained his singular focus of finding a medical cure for my situation, while my mother and brothers also remained focused on my care and well-being. Any day, I feared, they would grow weary of having their own lives stolen from them because of me. Any day, I feared, they would conclude enough was enough. Any day, I feared, they would abandon me in pursuit of their own lives. Any day, I feared, they would seek freedom from their imprisonment of my care.

The fears and apprehensions that are generated by a body that refuses to cooperate can take an adolescent mind into some dark places. And I've been into many of them.

Through the years, however, I began to see my family's relentless and unconditional devotion to my situation a little differently. I was becoming a little older and beginning to understand things a little better. I began to understand that unconditional love and unconditional faith meant, well, "unconditional." From our many travels in Ramadi, to Baghdad, to Jordan, to Russia, and eventually to the United States, I began to realize that any thoughts of abandonment or giving up existed only in my mind—no one else's.

I began to think about my predicament a little differently.

At Ali's high school graduation from Upper Merion High
School in 2012. Proudly displaying my brother's diploma,
my father was reminding me of how that would soon be me.
He was right.

I'm not sure when it happened, and I don't know if there
was a singular moment that gave me the epiphany, but it began
to happen.

Perhaps it happened when I realized that my father's focus
was not on my medical condition but on *resolving* my medical
condition. While I was obsessing on the problem, he was
focused on the solution.

Perhaps it was when I realized that my parents and my
brothers had long ago accepted the fact that our lives had

changed. And that I was the only one still living with the guilt of having disrupted our lives, as we once knew them. Perhaps it was when I realized they were prepared to adjust to whatever changes were necessary to deal with my condition, and that if I was dragging anybody down, it was not because of my physical condition; it was because of my attitude.

Perhaps it was after we moved to the U.S., and I realized there was technology that may or may not cure my medical condition, but that could give me the ability to engage and even impact other people's lives in some positive way.

Thanks to our insurance and the technology that was available in our schools, I was provided the ability to pretty much perform the same activities as any other student.

Four years later, it was my turn. This was my high school graduation in 2016.

I was provided a computer that could be controlled by an infrared equipped pair of glasses, which gave me "point and click" capabilities with my computer. Through those specially equipped glasses, combined with a straw that went into my mouth, and using a "sip and puff" technique, I could execute the right-click and left-click functions of the mouse. My computer also came with a voice dictation function, which enabled me to type and text using only my voice. Whether a two-line text or a twenty-page term paper, the technology I was afforded has been a major enabler in advancing my journey towards once again being functional and normal.

In short, I was provided the same computer capabilities that anyone else had, and, given my confinement, I became quite proficient very quickly. Truth be told, I was perhaps more proficient with the computer, then and today, than many full-functioning students or adults might be.

Perhaps it was then, when my power chair and computing technology put me on equal footing to perform my schoolwork as well as, and in many cases, better than other students, that I began to change my attitude.

Perhaps it was when I discovered the wonderous accomplishments of people like Dr. Stephen Hawking or Helen Keller, both of whom had suffered more debilitating circumstances than my own.

Perhaps it was when I realized that I still had my brain, and my ability to feel, and enjoy the simple wonders of life, like nature or like laughing and joking with my family. Perhaps it was then when I realized that those were really the major ingredients necessary to live a meaningful life.

I had my faith and the unwavering support of my family. Yet, for the longest time, it seemed, my sense of being was shaped by my disability. I was handicapped. I could not walk. I could not play sports. I wasn't normal like my brothers or like my classmates. Despite the support and encouragement I was receiving from my family and others, in my private moments, I could easily drift into a mindset of self-pity and regret and dwell on all the things I was unable to do.

It was as if, unless I could walk again, I could not live a full life. My mentality and sense of self were those of someone who was less than a whole person.

My change in attitude may have been spawned by a singular event or a combination of these or other events, but whatever it was and whenever it happened, it definitely began to happen.

I know what my parents and my brothers wanted for me. I know what my teachers and others wanted for me. But this was something that I could not rely on my parents or anyone else to do for me. This was ultimately mine and mine alone. And, I came to realize, it was a choice!

I could not choose what my body did or did not do. But I could choose what my mind could do.

I was a teenage quadriplegic, confined to a wheelchair, living in the very country that had inflicted this predicament on me, confronted with a choice few others are forced to confront at such an early age . . . to wallow in the sorrow of my predicament, or to accept it and make something from it.

For the longest time, my focus was on being cured or healed. And I defined being "healed" as walking again, playing soccer again . . . getting out of this wheelchair and living life again.

Being "healed," I finally learned, was as much a mental thing as it was a physical thing . . . maybe even more so. Being "healed" began to mean something very different to me.

I may or may not ever walk again. I'll have to rely on the wondrous advances in medical technology to make that decision. But I can be "healed." But, I realized, to do so would require a different mindset.

Instead of dwelling on all the things I could not do, I had

to focus on the things I could do. And amazingly, once I did, extraordinary things began to happen.

The Elmwood Park Zoo, which was located near our home in Norristown, Pennsylvania, served as a source of entertainment and education to the community about a variety of animal wildlife. Outside the community, the zoo is perhaps most known for being the home of Noah, the bald eagle that serves as the mascot of the local NFL franchise, the Philadelphia Eagles.

During the summer between my sophomore and junior years in high school, a math teacher I had at the time went out of his way to contact the volunteer coordinator at the zoo and see if there were any positions that would be a good fit for me. At the time, it seemed far-fetched that I could conceivably be given an actual job, especially one involving animals, which I loved.

But they agreed to interview me. After an extensive interview that lasted over an hour, I was given a position as an official greeter.

As amazing and unlikely as it seemed, it would be my face that visitors would first see as they came to check out the different animal species at the zoo. I was given a job that, given my love of animals, combined with my love of people, seemed to be perfect for me. I was given the role of educator, speaking to visitors at different animal stations at the zoo and talking about the various inhabitants. The volunteer position at the zoo was the best of both worlds; it gave me the opportunity to engage and educate people, and it was in an environment I loved.

Working as a volunteer at the Elmwood Park Zoo in 2016.

Was there something mystical that was causing these positive events to find me? Or was it as simple as focusing on making the best of the hand you are dealt? Whatever it was, I was getting my mindset in line with the faith that had been instilled in my brothers and me since birth.

Beyond being active and doing the things I enjoyed doing, my ultimate goal was to serve others. And my experience at the Elmwood Park Zoo was my first real taste of what that felt like.

I was beginning to get a real understanding of how faith worked. You don't simply believe and expect good things to happen to you. You have to have a purpose, believe in that purpose, actively work towards that purpose, *and* have faith.

Then, and only then, do those good things happen. That, I concluded, was and is the ultimate goal of the human spirit.

Volunteering at the zoo gave me that, and I wanted more. And it wouldn't be long before my faith and my desire to be of service to others found me yet again.

It found me when Steve, one of our neighbors, noticed me out on the street playing hockey. He was designing a home which he wished to be 100 percent handicapped accessible. Knowing my situation, he approached my father and asked if I could provide some guidance.

I knew nothing about home construction or about architectural design. But I certainly knew something about accessibility for the handicapped. It was from that perspective that I was able to provide insights and expertise that a non-handicapped individual could not provide. The man was extraordinarily friendly and engaging, which is something I will never forget. But something I will also never forget is the experience of being of value and service to another ... and being genuinely appreciated for my insights.

That was one of the most rewarding things I had experienced by that point in my life, and it once again solidified the lessons I was slowly learning. I was working with a man who was designing a home. Me! A disabled, wheelchair-bound quadriplegic, given the opportunity to be an "architectural design consultant."

That experience was yet another major building block in my transformation from one who dwelled on my disabilities to one who dwelled on my abilities. These childhood and adolescent experiences may have had nothing to do with my ultimate livelihood or my life's work, but they had everything to do with helping me discover that I could be of value to others, whether it was while standing or from a wheelchair.

I dared myself to dream. I dared to believe I could actually be of value to others. Me, a wheelchair-bound quadriplegic who required assistance in feeding himself or going to the bathroom, would dare have the audacity to believe he could be active and help others. What was I thinking?

I reminded myself that I was smart. I reminded myself that I engaged others easily. I had a desire to help others. I had a variety of interests, and I had boundless curiosity. After graduating from high school, I took one more unthinkable step: I enrolled in college.

One of those good things happened to me back during my second year in middle school after moving to the U.S. I was in the seventh grade, probably 11 or 12 years old. A woman who worked with my father at an allergy clinic told him of her grandson who was confined to a wheelchair because of cerebral palsy. We learned that he played in a floor hockey league at a local YMCA.

With my power hockey teammates, Liam Miller and
Jake Saxton, in 2017.

My father took me to meet with the man who ran the league. I was obviously excited, but I was apprehensive at the prospect of becoming actively engaged in a sports activity. I had not been active in any fashion since the bombing incident, and that was over four years ago. Even the thought of participating in a sports activity was both thrilling and terrifying. But, I knew it was something I wanted to do.

It was a way for me to be active. It enabled me to befriend more young people of varying ages who were all dealing with a variety of disabilities. It reminded me that I was not alone. The only requirement for participation was that I must have a power wheelchair, which I did.

In action with the Philadelphia Flyers Power Play Hockey League

I ended up really enjoying my time attending power hockey practice every other weekend or so. I even once participated in a tournament that saw players converging on our area from all over North America. I got to meet new people, learn a lot about others' disabilities, be active, and get out of the house. And all the while, I was not focused on my disability. I was focused on participating in competitive sports with others.

I was now living the life that every other red-blooded teenager wishes to live ... actively engaging others. Sharing with others. Being one of the gang ... competing, laughing, and joking. I was in a new country, playing a new sport, and living a new life.

In 2018, our team won the North America Power Hockey Cup ... the Stanley Cup of power hockey.

Playing in the Philadelphia Power Play hockey league was, without a doubt, one of those events. It made me forget all about my situation. It made me feel like I did when I was a young boy in Iraq kicking around a soccer ball. Amazingly, rather than dwelling on my pain and suffering, I was experiencing life. I was becoming a whole human being.

While hockey has become a favorite pastime of mine, it is only one of the positive things that found me once I began to focus on living as opposed to being disabled. I was introduced to an opportunity where I could actually be of service to others.

When we immigrated to the United States, each of my brothers and I were confronted with the task of continuing our educations. My oldest brother, Mohammed, had already been accepted to a university in Jordan at the time, and had to adjust his plans quickly. My other brothers, Ali and Mustafa, would soon follow suit. The transition for each of them began at Montgomery County Community College in nearby Blue Bell, Pennsylvania.

After graduation from high school, I was confronted with the same issue that confronts all high school graduates . . . what to do with the rest of my life? As a quadriplegic, the question was a little more complicated for me, but the alternative of just hanging around and doing nothing was not in my family's DNA. There is a favorite expression of mine that says, "You cannot control your past, but you can control your future." It was time for me to put that expression to work.

Following in my brothers' footsteps, in 2019 I graduated from Montgomery County Community College.

By this time in my life, I had gotten out and done things. I was able to play power ice hockey, a variation of the sport, but in power wheelchairs. I worked as a volunteer at the local zoo. I had served as a consultant on the design of a home that was fully accessible to the handicapped. The technology of my wheelchair aided both my mobility and my communications. As I had learned to do so many times earlier in my life, I had to ask the question . . . "Is there any reason you cannot do this?" The answer was no.

And I concluded, I had the choice to find ways to leverage those qualities to help others or to live a life of self-pity and regret.

When you put those options in front of you, "A" or "B," the choice seems simple. Of course you want to choose doing things and helping others, rather than living a life of self-pity and regret. But it is a choice that is simple to make, but difficult to sustain. It is one, I learned, that requires daily, sometimes hourly, and sometimes, minute-by-minute reminders. It is one that requires the utmost discipline. Staying positive and staying focused, when you can't even feed yourself, is hard work . . . perhaps the hardest thing I'll ever have to do.

Since the age of 8, I had been confined to nothing but hospital beds and wheelchairs. One moment, I'm playing with my brothers, and the next, I'm lying in the back of a van and given up for dead. By the fluke of being in our front yard instead of in school that morning, because it was our turn to attend school in the afternoon, and because I was standing where I was at the time, this was my fate.

Confinement to a hospital bed or a wheelchair gives you ample opportunity to feel sorry for yourself, or to be angry at the cards you've been dealt. And I admit, I have had both of those feelings, along with thousands of the "why me" pity parties. But my faith and my family would not allow any of those thoughts or feelings to persist.

Both of those taught me that it's not where you are or your circumstance that governs your existence. It is *why* you're here . . . and we all have a *why*. We all have a purpose. I was still sorting through my purpose, but I knew I had one.

I once believed I was immobile, unlike others. Then I discovered the magic of power wheelchairs. I once believed I would not be able to go to school like others. Then I discovered the magic of "smart" wheelchairs. I once believed I was handicapped. Then I discovered the magic of my brain.

I was not immobile. I simply had other means of mobility. I was not unable to go to school and learn like others. I just had other means of learning. I was only as handicapped as I allowed myself to believe I was handicapped. And I was determined to never allow myself to believe that.

Admittedly, there are good days and bad days.

There are times when I am totally down and unable to muster the energy to be positive and would rather feel sorry for myself. There are times when I can't do things right on the first try, and I get angry and frustrated. There are times when I want to lash out at the Americans who did this to me, or at the world, or even at God for allowing this to happen to me.

But then I come back to something else I finally discovered . . . God gives *all* of us challenges. This just happens to be mine.

There are those who do not have homes to sleep in, or food to eat, or families who support them. Here, in the richest country on Earth, there are those who have health predicaments as bad as or worse than my own, and who don't have the means to get proper health care. Even those who seem to have it all have their challenges. Theirs may not be visible to the casual observer, but they are there.

This is simply my challenge. And what I do with it, is my choice.

Celebrating my junior college commencement with my English Professor, Marc Schuster

Another thing I learned is that the more I focused on the things I could do, rather than the things I could not do, the more those good things would find me. Our faith tells us that, but all of us have to learn that in our own way.

. . . and with my brother Mustafa.

Still today I have to remind myself of what I can do versus what I cannot do. I am constantly reminded that the choice to focus on the positive versus the negative is easy to make but difficult to sustain. But the more I do it, the easier it is to sustain.

And the way it is reinforced is through nature. My time connecting with animals and the outdoors is my sustenance. It is those times that remind me of my faith and the love and support of my family. It is those times when I am outside taking in the various sights, sounds, and smells that the world has to offer that I may be the happiest and most at peace.

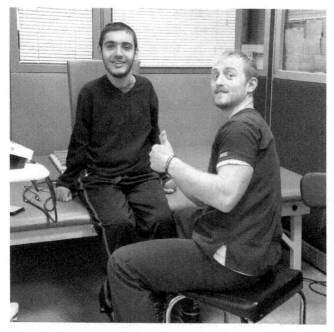

With Chris, in one of my therapy sessions in 2019 at
the Magee Rehab Center in Philadelphia.

In fact, perhaps the ultimate irony of the many ironies of
our long and tortuous journey over the past decade is that our
entire family has found peace in this country.

Given that we've now made a life for ourselves here in
the United States, the very place that brought war to our
homeland, I am often asked how I can be positive, given what
I've experienced. I've been asked about things like my faith and
the idea of forgiveness. How is it, the question is frequently
posed, that you can be at peace living in the very country that
was responsible for your predicament? How is it you can be
so understanding and not have hate or resentment toward

Americans? After all, I am reminded, if the U.S. had never launched a war against Iraq, you would likely be walking today.

Perhaps the answer to those questions is even more perplexing, especially given all the fanfare and political commentary about the Muslim faith. Over the past few years, there has been much noise about "Muslim radicals" and those who have attempted to co-opt the Muslim faith to justify violence. Our faith, and that of the vast majority of Muslims, is grounded in the spirit of peace and understanding, as reflected in a standard Muslim greeting, "Peace be unto you."

That faith has been the backbone of my family's and my perseverance throughout our ordeal over the past decade, and it will continue to carry us forward. It is that faith that allows me to stay focused on living my life without hate in my heart.

Derek, another of my therapists at Magee Rehab Facility in 2019.

I could easily go through my days filled with hate, fighting with God, and cursing the heavens, depressingly questioning why it is that I ended up this way. But that simply does no good. It doesn't cure my inability to walk. It doesn't give our family back our home that was destroyed. It doesn't give my parents, my brothers, or me the futures to which we had aspired. And it most definitely does not return our homeland to the country that it once was.

Our family is very religious. And as clichéd as it may sound, a part of our religious beliefs is that everything happens for a reason; and it is our job to discover and pursue that reason.

From my father's perspective, and my own, we are not here to hate or seek revenge. We are here to give firsthand testimony to the savagery and perils of war and the wisdom and the need for peace.

PART II

The Rest of the Story

CHAPTER 10

My Family

THE DESTRUCTION OF our home and life as we knew it in Iraq affected not only me, but my entire family. My paralysis was the driving force that took us from Iraq, to Jordan, to Russia, and ultimately to the United States. Little did I appreciate at the time, my saga was their saga, too.

My parents and my brothers literally gave up the lives we were all enjoying in Iraq in order to accommodate my situation. And, they never seemed to question it. It was just what families do!

What must that have been like for them? At the time, I was pretty much preoccupied with my own circumstances. I was just happy they were there with me. They were what kept me going. But, during those days, I never gave much thought to how they were affected by the situation. Now, as I look back, I have to say it was the most amazing act of selflessness I can ever imagine.

My father was forced to abandon the vision he once held so dear to have us grow together and spend our lives together with our families in Ramadi. He was forced to redefine and re-establish his career and his entire way of life in a foreign land in order to find the best health care he could for his son.

The same is true for my mother. She, too, was a prominent physician in Iraq. She completely abandoned her career just to take care of me. All that schooling, all that work she put into her work as an ophthalmologist . . . gone. Caring for me became her new career.

And my brothers . . . my brothers were my role models. As an 8-year-old, whatever they did, I tried to emulate. I vividly remember those days when we would play football—what Americans call soccer—and other games together. I was the little brother trying to keep up. Though I was in the very early stages of my education, they were all in the midst of their schooling with their friends. Then, in the blink of an eye, that was all taken from them.

I'm sure they had dreams, too—dreams that most likely did not include traipsing all over the globe as my father went searching for care for their little brother. Yet, seemingly without question, they complied. They adjusted to their lives during those two months in Baghdad, and then to their lives in Jordan. And more dramatically, they adjusted to becoming Americans, in the very country that had turned their lives upside down.

Finding the proper care for their little brother evidently took precedence over whatever dreams and visions they may have had for themselves.

Now, after more than a decade since that horrible day, I am able to reflect on how that single moment had such a devastating effect not just on my own life, but the lives of my entire family. I marvel at how they adjusted to the continuous series of events, but I couldn't help but wonder how they adjusted so well. What were they going through as the circumstances continually changed? I wanted their perspective.

Much of what they saw in those days, I was too young, too

unconscious, or too unaware of the situation to see. As I was confined to my hospital bed, undergoing a myriad of treatments and surgical procedures, consciously and unconsciously, the rest of the family had to somehow try to maintain some sense of normalcy in their own lives.

What must it have been like for them... following the saga of my recovery, first being near death in Ramadi, then in hospital beds in Baghdad, and then in Jordan, all while continuing to go to school, go grocery shopping, maintain a household, and all the other things families have to do? What must they have thought when they learned that the best health care for me would be found, of all places, in America?

What I came to realize is that, with the exception of the physical effects I experienced, they have a story as dramatic as my own. Their stories are a mirror image of my story. Yet, theirs is a perspective I was unable to see. Theirs represents the other side of my story.

What did they see during those horrific days? What were they feeling? How did they cope?

This part of my story is not about me. It is about my father, my mother, and my three brothers, and the lives and the situations they were thrown into, because of me.

These, as they have shared with me, are their stories.

CHAPTER 11

A Father's Perspective

Me and my father.

WEDNESDAY, MARCH 22, 2006, began as a normal day for my father. He and my mom went to work as usual. They planned to return home and take my brothers and me to our afternoon school session, as usual. But they never got that chance. Around 10:30 a.m. that morning, all my father had worked for his entire life, all the plans he had for his wife and his family, all he had known and enjoyed, would be blown away by that bomb.

I know what that was like for me. I can even imagine what that must have been like for my brothers. But I have great difficulty imagining what that was like for my father. He had a family for which he was responsible. He didn't have the luxury of just worrying about himself. He had a wife and four sons to take care of. Up until that day, our lives were going according to his plan. To have all he had been working toward simply taken away on that morning is impossible for me to comprehend.

When Father and Mother awoke, the two of them had some time together before my brothers and I woke up. My brothers, Mohammed (16 years), Mustafa (14 years), and Ali (12 years) and I, 8 at the time, were all still sound asleep, he remembers. The schools in Iraq had separate sessions for the male and female students and rotated between morning and afternoon sessions. On this day, the male students were scheduled to attend their classes in the afternoon.

He said he first woke Mohammed and told him he and my mom were going to work at Al-Ramadi General Hospital and would return to take us to school in the afternoon. He said they left around 8:30 a.m. and arrived at the hospital shortly thereafter. Their day, he recalls, began with their regular routine.

Since the war had begun in March of 2003, fighting between the militia and the American troops had become a normal part of our day. But on this day, he recalled, it seemed quiet. That was until a member of the nursing staff came to his clinic and told him that fighting had erupted in the area, and there had been explosions and gunfire exchanges. He had said, "There are many casualties in the emergency room."

As per normal protocol, my father proceeded to the ER to assist. He witnessed a chaotic scene. The ER was flooded with many injured civilians and their family members, in addition to the medical staff. Since ambulances were unavailable, the casualties were typically transported by neighbors in their private vehicles, which added to the crowded situation.

He remembers almost immediately seeing our neighbor's 9-year-old son among the injured. He was unconscious with shrapnel penetrating his chest in the area of his heart. He said they immediately transported him to the operating theater in the ER, where a cardiovascular surgeon tried to save him. Unfortunately, it was too late. The boy was a close friend of ours. My father remembers being sad and upset and leaving the operating theater with tears in his eyes.

When he returned to the ER, he said, he experienced an even bigger shock. He saw my brother, Mustafa, standing in the midst of the chaos. "What are you doing here?" he remembers asking Mustafa. He said Mustafa's response was perhaps the most devastating reply he could imagine.

"My three brothers were injured by the bomb," Mustafa told him.

With that, my father said he immediately began to scan the crowded scene, looking for his sons. He said he first saw Mohammed, who had multiple shrapnel injuries to his back and lower legs. He was conscious and seemed not seriously injured. My father said Mohammed told him, 'Dad, I am OK. Check on Hisham!"

He then saw Ali, my third-oldest brother. He was lying on another bed with what appeared to be serious wounds to his gluteal area. He was bleeding profusely, but he, too, seemed to be conscious and OK. He, too, told my father, "Dad, I am fine. Check on Hisham."

As Ali and Mohammed were being attended to by others, he said he began furiously looking for me. However, he could not find me on any of the beds in the crowded ER. "Where is Hisham?" he remembered frantically asking. He described feeling a sense of panic. The ER was crowded. The scene was pure bedlam, and his youngest son seemed nowhere to be found.

Eventually, he said, he spotted me. I was not in one of the beds, but lying on the floor, as if, he described, I had been discarded like bed linens. He said I was pale, unconscious, not breathing, and had no peripheral pulse. Though a well-trained physician, he was also a father, confronted face to face with a critically injured son. I cannot imagine what he must have been feeling.

He described how he leaned toward me to check my carotid pulse. He said he could detect a faint pulse, which increased his sense of urgency. "He is alive," my father screamed. "Please help me."

He said the medical staff responded immediately. As I was still unconscious, they began efforts to resuscitate me, administering IV fluids and blood. I was later told I was bleeding profusely.

The decision was made to take me to the operating theater, where they would attempt to stop the bleeding. Shrapnel had penetrated much of my neck, including my jugular vein, which was the major cause of the bleeding.

Until this moment, I was told, my mother was completely unaware of what had happened to my brothers and me. My father asked a member of the medical staff to call her to come to the ER. Upon being informed of what had happened she proceeded immediately to the emergency room. When she saw Mohammed and Ali injured and bleeding, she immediately collapsed in anguish.

Unfortunately, my father had little opportunity to comfort her, as he was accompanying the surgeons to take me to the operating theater. She remained with my brothers. Meanwhile, my father, being an allergist and not a surgeon, was left to wait outside the OR in an adjacent waiting room with our neighbors and family friends as the surgeons worked on me.

After about an hour, my father said, the surgeon stepped out the operating theater to tell him they were able to stop the bleeding and that my condition was stable. I was moved to the recovery room, but was still unconscious, breathing rapidly and gasping for air. More testing would be necessary.

This is when the medical staff were confronted with another of the many consequences of war . . . a lack of supplies and equipment.

I was told I needed a CT scan, which the hospital had once had. It worked prior to the war but stopped working afterward due to the hospital being unable to maintain them. Those machines were useless. The next best option, which would be limited in value, was to have X-rays taken. I was told I was then transferred to the radiology department, where X-rays were conducted to my chest and abdomen areas. The X-rays could not detect any abnormalities.

Given the absence of additional diagnostic equipment, there was nothing further that could be done locally. That is when my father was advised to take me to Baghdad. The capital city had better health care and diagnostic facilities. This, I was told, was some four to five hours since the incident.

How could he possibly transfer me from Ramadi to Baghdad, my father remembered wondering. The capitol city was seventy miles away, and we were in a war zone. Though he had yet to have a plan as to how he would be able to do it, he told my mother he was taking me to Baghdad. She would need to remain in Ramadi with my two other injured brothers, Mohammed and Ali, and my third brother, Mustafa, who had escaped injury. At the time, I was still unconscious, breathing very hard, and gasping for air.

Now, to the question of how. The best way to transport

me would obviously be by ambulance. That was the first of the many challenges he would have to overcome. He had to secure an ambulance, find a driver, get gas, all in the midst of a war, and all with no communications. There were no cellphone connections and no other means to make additional arrangements.

Miraculously, with the invaluable help from his colleagues in the hospital, two hours later, the ambulance was there and ready to go. For good measure, one of our neighbors and a friend accompany us in the ambulance. I was told that around 5 p.m., some seven hours after the explosion had occurred, we embarked for Baghdad.

Up to this point, my cervical spine had not been examined. In the chaos of the circumstances, given that the primary focus had been my excessive bleeding, compounded by the lack of equipment to perform further testing, that area of my body had not been thoroughly examined. Additionally, there was the urgency to get me to Baghdad.

Under normal circumstances, that seventy-mile trip would have been made in seventy-five to ninety minutes. Given the war situation, the trip took us five hours! Every couple of miles, we encountered a military checkpoint, and every one of them involved a thorough search of our vehicle. I was told that seeing me in my unconscious condition and being on oxygen didn't seem to matter to the American soldiers. The Americans were determined to execute a detailed examination of the vehicle and its contents. They inspected every vehicle, ours included, as in their eyes it could be transporting militia or contraband.

Additionally, we were restricted to traveling backroads. The main roads, they told my father, were reserved for military vehicles only. Any obstacle that could have impaired our efforts to get me to the hospital that night, I was told, seemed to occur.

The trip had taken so long that at some point we ran out

of oxygen, and I was gasping for air. My father said he feared losing me before we reached Baghdad. He had to resort to using an Ambu bag to keep me breathing. An Ambu bag is a medical device that requires manual compressions to give resuscitative breaths.

I later learned from my father that I was on oxygen and that I needed to be resuscitated every ten to fifteen minutes throughout the duration of the trip to the hospital in Baghdad. Those had to have been tense moments.

It was around 10 p.m. when we finally arrived at the medical facility in Baghdad. The hospital we went to was a teaching hospital where my father had received his medical training and gone through his residency program. Fortunately, he knew many people there, including teachers, colleagues, and even students he had once taught at Al-Anbar Medical College.

Once we arrived, they immediately took me to the emergency room, and just as quickly, my father began reaching out to any of his friends and colleagues he thought could help. He called a close friend of his who was a general surgeon and former classmate back in Ramadi. He said the friend remembered playing with me when he visited us at our home during his time in Ramadi.

When my father's friend first saw me, my father said, he immediately began crying. The gregarious, carefree boy the doctor had once played with when he would come to our home in Ramadi was now pale, unconscious, and gasping for air. It was this man who discovered my condition. After examining me, with tears in his eyes, he hugged my father and said, "Abdul, your son has a spinal cord injury!"

In looking back at when the bomb explosion first occurred, the way I was transported to the hospital in Ramadi and again while in the hospital had a great impact on my spinal cord injury and disability.

It was then, almost thirteen hours after the explosion, that my father learned the full extent of my injuries. They conducted a CT scan and put a cervical collar on my neck, and I was admitted to the intensive care unit. It was almost 1 a.m., the following morning, and I was still unconscious and now on a ventilator.

There is a movie about the allied invasion of Normandy, France, during World War II called *The Longest Day*. March 22, 2006, was most assuredly the longest day in my father's life. And this was just the beginning. It was not only his longest day, but was the first day in his life of having a son who was now a quadriplegic; a wife and three other sons back in Ramadi; and a life he had spent a lifetime creating for himself and his family that had been destroyed.

What next?

During the war, there were no cellphones or internet or other means of communications. This meant there was no way of knowing what was happening to my brothers and my mom. Likewise, they did not know what was happening with us. They did not know what my father had learned about my condition.

My father remembered his wife calling him using a satellite phone one of our neighbors had provided her. My mother's first question was, "How is Hisham? Is Hisham dead?" She could not stop crying. Likewise, he was asking her, "How are Mohammed and Ali doing?"

We had just endured the longest, most agonizing day of our lives, and the journey we would be undertaking from this point forward, had just begun.

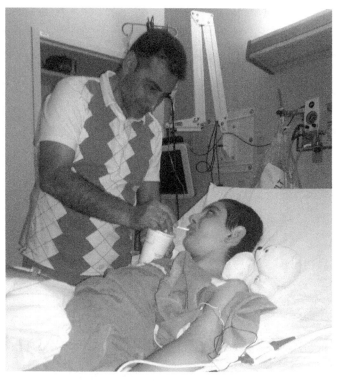

My father in his usual position of looking after me after
my spinal surgery in 2013.

CHAPTER 12
A Mother's Nightmare

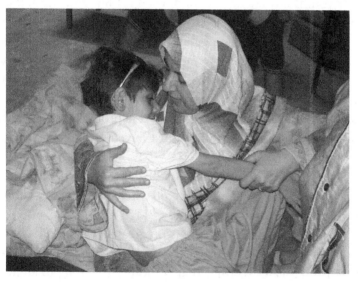

Me with my mother.

U PON REFLECTION, I am constantly reminded of all that I lost on that fateful day. Having been confined to a wheelchair for over a decade now, the reminders are with me from the moment I awake each morning to the moment I fall asleep each night. I am also, however, reminded of the enormous adjustments my family has been required to make to accommodate my circumstances.

We are now residing in a country we would not have chosen. My father has leveraged his medical training to find meaningful employment in the U.S., but that, too, would not have been of his choosing. My brothers were taken from their friends and dreams of growing up in our home country of Iraq to find themselves in an environment dramatically different than what they would have chosen. Every day, I'm thankful for their youthful resilience to not only adjust but flourish in their new lives here in America.

Perhaps the greatest anguish I feel when I think about the changes and sacrifices my family has been forced to make because of my circumstance is when I think about my mother. There is a saying that the most terrible grief imaginable is a mother seeing her child suffering. I'll probably never fully comprehend what my mother must have been going through during those times.

From the unthinkable horrors of that day, to the around-the-world saga she had to endure, all while caring for her family as my father pursued his relentless search for my recovery.

There is an adage that there is no greater love than the love a mother has for her children. The parallel to that adage, is that there is no greater sacrifice than a mother is willing to endure for her children. My mother has lived that sacrifice every day since March 22, 2006.

My father has parlayed the medical training and his skills as a physician into a prosperous position with a medical firm here in the U.S. He travels throughout this country, engaging with other medical practitioners on a daily basis. The career he enjoys today is not of his original choosing, but it allows for a continued application of his training and skills as an allergist.

My brothers, whom I have looked up to since my earliest days as a child playing with them in the neighborhoods of Ramadi, have also made extraordinary adjustments. Their youthful resilience, combined with their unquestioned devotion to do what's right in the care of their little brother, equipped them to adapt, perhaps as well as any of us. In a matter of months, it seemed that they integrated themselves into a new country, a new language, and a new way of life. They appeared to seamlessly translate the same popularity and success they had been realizing in the schools in Iraq and Jordan to their American friends and education system.

By contrast, my mother enjoyed no such transfer. The medical training she had received to become a physician in Iraq came to a halt that day. The comforts of our home in Ramadi, in which she cooked and cleaned for us tirelessly, came to a halt that day. There was no such transition of her medical skills from her position she enjoyed in the hospital in Ramadi. Her role as caretaker for the residential compound she and my father were preparing for their four sons was not to be.

As of that day, her career and everything she and my father had envisioned for us came to a halt. She took on a new career that day, which was the continuous around-the-clock care of her youngest son, while continuing to provide a home for her family as we transitioned from Ramadi, to Baghdad, to Jordan, and eventually to the U.S.

The career and life she had known and envisioned before that day would be no more, and it appeared she never once complained about it. My father's and my brothers' sacrifices, it seemed, went from Option A to a less-than-desirable Option B. My mother's, it seemed, went from Option A to no option.

I became her default Option B, and it seemed she never looked back.

On the day of the explosion, when my brothers and I were brought into the hospital, I was told that my mother collapsed from the overwhelming weight of the moment when she learned of our situation. Learning that three of her four sons had received injuries from the explosion, and one of the three was on the brink of death, is a burden that hopefully the rest of us will never know. My mother was taken to a private area to regain her strength and her composure, all at a time when my father was preoccupied with the issue of my very survival.

When later that day it was determined that my father would have to transport me to Baghdad for further treatment, my mother was tasked to stay behind with my brothers to oversee their treatment. In what was undoubtedly the worst day of her life, she did not even get the luxury of being consoled by her husband. In a time of war and the chaos that it brings, there is no time to reflect or to grieve. In a matter of hours, she had gone from hearing the devastating news of the explosion and our injuries to bidding my father and me goodbye while she looked after my brothers.

She would not fully grasp the magnitude of my situation until five days later when she and my brothers joined my father and me in Baghdad. Only then was she brought face-to-face with the impact of my injuries. Seeing me in the intensive care unit at the hospital in Baghdad may have been as devastating to my mother as the initial news of the explosion days earlier. I try to imagine what it must have been like for her to see her eight-year-old baby boy lying there in a hospital bed with all types of tubes coming out of him as he was hooked up to various machines. She was forced to be strong and keep it together as no mother should have to do.

Another woman who had been visiting her sister in the

intensive care unit of the hospital noticed how strong my mom was in dealing with the care of her son. She asked my mother to give her some strength and patience in helping her with her sister. My mother was not only caring for me, but helping other families as well.

Those first few days after the bombing had to have been the most difficult days of my mother's life. Her faith was tested in perhaps the cruelest of ways, and she stood tall—just as she has every day since then.

My mom saw a cruel irony in the circumstances in which we found ourselves in those days. Before that fateful day, and even before the beginning of the war with the U.S., she told of a very different Iraq. "We lived a very peaceful existence in a peaceful city," she said. "Everyone helped each other," she recalled.

"While the outside world viewed Saddam as a brutal dictator, the average Iraqi civilian felt pretty safe during his regime. Certainly, our country had its problems," she said, "just like many other countries, but the incidence of sniper attacks, explosions, roadside bombs, fighting between the Americans and the militia, and kidnappings were almost unheard of during Saddam's time in power." She explained how being afraid of Saddam also meant people were afraid to commit crimes, hence the feeling of relative safety under his rule. "Once the war started," she said, "things began to change drastically."

She told horrific stories of how our family and neighbors were subjected to a virtually lawless environment. She said many teachers were killed. She described an incident in which a child was killed by a sniper because he was holding a toy gun. She told of how soldiers would burst into hospitals looking for militia insurgents, even coming into operating rooms. There were unannounced raids in the middle of the night, when American troops were in search of militants. Families were forced to sit outside their own houses for two to three hours at a time, or even overnight while the troops conducted their searches.

Our family was not immune to that lawless environment. We had multiple incidents of Americans breaking into our home to search for militants. During those occasions, however, my mother did not hesitate to speak her mind. During one of those unannounced middle-of-the-night raids, she told the troops that searching civilian homes in the middle of the night was not the way to go about things if they wanted to win over the Iraqi people.

As strong as my mother was during those early days of the war, her strength was never more evident than in the aftermath of the bombing that destroyed our family home and almost destroyed me.

I was a frightened, paralyzed 8-year-old, trying to make sense of the horrific events of our situation. My fear was accompanied by deep bouts of depression. Not only had we lost our home, but I had lost my mobility. My world was closing in on me during those days. As devastated as my mother must have been during those days, she never let it show. She constantly reminded me that crying and worrying won't solve the problem. I needed to be strong and rely on my faith and the determination of my family.

"We hope one day it will be OK," she says. "But for now, this is our life. We must accept it and move forward." Her combination of tough love, faith, and determination was what kept me going when I needed it most.

She would point out that there were thousands of children in Iraq right then who were alone. Thousands more were orphaned because of the war. I eventually began to realize that, unlike me, these children don't have wonderful people in their lives to help keep their spirits up. I am lucky that way. I would soon come to realize that though I lost something, I have a wonderfully supportive family and a lot of good in my life. There were countless people in Iraq who had suffered injuries similar to or more severe than mine and did not have even a manual wheelchair, or any support from the government.

My mother has a devout faith and a strong belief system. She is a major part of the fabric that has helped us come to grips with the reality of our situation and live each day thankful that we're all still alive and together.

It is her constant presence that guided me through those early nightmarish days, and it is her presence, even to this day, that reminds me that I am not alone.

CHAPTER 13

My Brothers

MY FATHER HAS always been the foundation of our family. He set the tone and the standards for how we lived our lives back in Ramadi, and it was his guidance that navigated us through our saga and where we are today. My mother was his perfect partner. She served as the perfect counterbalance. What my father provided in terms of guidance and direction, she provided in terms of love and nourishment.

The interpretation and application of that guidance, however, came from my brothers. How I internalized that guidance on a day-to-day basis came from them. They were my role models.

I am the youngest of four brothers. From my earliest memories, I was the tag-along. I was the little brother who struggled to keep up. I was the subject of my brothers' razzing and, many times, the butt of their jokes. They challenged me to try to do things I wasn't sure I could do. But I was determined to do them. Whatever it was, if they could do it, I wanted to do it. If I could endure what they dished out, I believed I could handle anything. They made me stronger, faster, tougher.

They were my earliest heroes and my earliest caretakers.

When our parents were at work at the hospital, it was my brothers who looked after me. When I fell, it was my brothers who picked me up. When I cried, it was my brothers who wiped my tears. They would challenge me to try new things, but if I failed or was afraid, they would comfort me.

Growing up with my three older brothers, our lives were full of adventure, excitement, and happiness. We knew we were in the midst of a war, but that was not about us. We were aware of the presence of American troops, but, other than the occasional disruptions of late-night searches of our home and stories of gunfire and skirmishes, we were doing our best to just be kids being kids.

In those days, we could not have dreamed that the lives we were enjoying could have been destroyed by one of those skirmishes. We could not have imagined that my brothers and I would have been subjected to the explosion that would injure them and put them in the position of having to save my life.

But that's exactly what happened.

All four of us were subjected to the explosion, yet each of us suffered differing effects. And we each had differing perspectives on what happened. Given that I was rendered unconscious by the blast, it is my brothers who were obviously able to recount and reconstruct the events of that morning far better than I.

From my oldest brother, Mohammed, who was 16, to my second brother, Mustafa, who was 14 and amazingly not injured, to my third brother, Ali, who was 12, theirs is a perspective both my parents and I were eager to hear.

This is their stories of the events of that morning and the journey that followed.

Mohammed

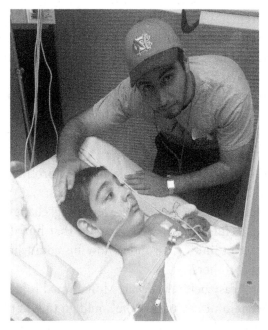

Mohammed, brandishing his University of North Carolina baseball cap, reassuring me during my spinal surgery in 2013.

With me being the youngest of four brothers, and Mohammed being the oldest, he and I were very close. He was always looking out for me, for as long as I can remember. I think back to times when I might be picked on by other kids. I could always count on him if I ever ran into trouble.

Mohammed has never been a violent person. As best as I can remember, he has only been in two fights, and both of them were to protect his brothers. If people called him names or tried to start something, he never responded. But if it was one of us, it was a different story. He took the role of big brother very seriously.

In describing our earlier times together, he said of me, "Hisham was full of energy. It almost felt like he was always running. I remember taking him on bike rides and he would sit behind me and hold on tightly. I was happy knowing he felt safe with me." I have always felt safe with Mohammed, even in our darkest days.

For example, when attending school in the midst of war, and caught in a crossfire, with bullets flying all around as everyone was scrambling to evacuate, he was corralling his brothers to safety. As the rest of the students were running from the gunfire and explosions, Mohammed was leading his brothers through sheltered alleyways to safety.

On March 22, 2006, however, everything changed. While we are all grateful to have even survived that horrific day, to this day, he continues to wonder how he could have better protected his brothers.

Life wasn't easy before the war, Mohammed told me, but it was safe. He reminisced of how we could go to school without the fear of dying. There were issues with electricity and water, he told me, but we managed. Our parents would work at the hospital during school, and our dad would work in his clinic after the hospital. We always had lunch and dinner together as a family.

He told me how in 2003, when American troops entered our city, he was optimistic that their presence would make things better for us. He said, "I watched with my friends as the U.S. military entered our city. Some of the tribal leaders welcomed them to their homes and invited them for food. We didn't really know what to expect. People were optimistic that maybe life could change for the better, but we were wrong. While things were quiet in the beginning for the most part, a shift began to occur.

"There were random house searches in the middle of the

night. If you didn't open your front door when the military knocked, it would get kicked in, blown up, or run through by a humvee. That is when people began to retaliate. Homes in Iraq are sacred. The U.S. soldiers either didn't understand or even care about our culture."

After living in the U.S., and having gotten to know the American people, Mohammed told me, he was more certain of that than ever. "Most people who signed up for the war," he said, "didn't know what they were getting into. Some thought they're going in to save the country. But once they realized the reality was different, they couldn't mentally recover."

Mohammed's memories of those days are very vivid. As he reflected on those times, he continued, "I can't count the number of times we were wakened at two, three, or four o'clock in the morning with an M16 pointed at our heads and asked to leave because they were conducting a random search. I remember one time when an American soldier saw our Mickey Mouse poster on the wall and made a friendly comment about it. I smiled and nodded at the comment, but quickly remembered the reality that we could be shot at any moment.

"I know I saw fear in their eyes as well; they were fighting a losing battle in an unjust war against the unknown. Yet still, as a teenager in pajamas in my bedroom at three o'clock in the morning sitting between soldiers all decked out in gear from head to toe, I didn't think I was a threat."

He reflected on his life as a normal Iraqi teenager, trying to live a normal life in the middle of a war.

"Our normal day in school began with us calling our friends on each road to make sure it was safe. That was before the phones were taken out; then it was just a gamble, but so were our lives there. Finishing a 'normal' school day didn't always happen. Our school was located next to a government building that served as a military outpost, which made it common for us to get caught in battles.

"When we heard the first explosion, we knew immediately to start packing our things, because we knew that would be followed by a constant barrage of bullets and explosions. I felt the bullets go by my ear and saw them land in front me as I held my brother Mustafa closer and kept running home. Now that I think about it, even our home was unsafe since it was riddled with bullets, including our bedroom. That was the life of an Iraqi teenager in the middle of a war zone.'

He also told me of an occasion when he and our brother Mustafa were walking to a nearby restaurant after school to get a sandwich with friends. As they were leaving, he said, they heard gunfire, which alarmed the nearby American soldiers. He described how they ran past the two of them with guns aimed and shoving Mustafa in the process. He said he saw his brother's eyes fill with fear as they continued their walk home. After that incident, he said, they never returned to that spot.

When asked why they would even go to a dangerous area to get food in the first place, his response was, "*Everywhere* was a dangerous area. There were no safe areas. Life had to go on. Do you think any teenager chooses to go into a dangerous area? We just wanted what every kid in the world wants . . . to have a life where our conversations weren't about warfare and wondering which of our friends was going to make it to school that day."

He said, if a kid were absent from school on a given day, the first question the other kids would ask was, "Is he still alive?"

Being the oldest of the brothers, Mohammed, like my parents, experienced more of the horrors of the war than I did. He told of how one of his best friends watched his father lying in his own blood, dying from a gunshot wound just a few feet away from his house. He remembered sitting with his friend in the funeral home, wondering what he could say or do to ease his friend's agony. He concluded that the only thing he could do was simply sit and listen, being there for his friend. "That was our life during the war," he said.

Yet, through it all, he said, we still continued to live our lives, but ever vigilant, ever fearful. He described waiting every night for our dad to return home from his clinic and listening closely for the sound of his car, which he had learned to recognize. "With that sound," he told me, "we could breathe a sigh of relief and have our dinner. We would never know when our father would get home because it always depended on how many patients he had, and which roads were closed at the time."

With war, nothing is certain, Mohammed reflected. And uncertainty breeds paranoia and fear of the worst. He described one occasion when his paranoia and fear of the worst reached its peak.

"One time I dropped Dad off at his clinic because he was planning to take a cab home. I waited for him as usual, but when it started getting late, you start thinking about the worst when you live in a war zone. Even though I tried to remain positive and calm about the situation, the later it got, the more worried I became.

"I decided I was going to take matters into my own hands. I got into the car and backed out of our garage. When our neighbors saw me, they thought I was crazy since there was a curfew and we were not allowed to drive after a certain hour. I might not have gotten a ticket if I got caught, but I could have very easily been shot! At the time, that didn't matter to me. All I was thinking was that our dad wasn't home.

"Our neighbor got in the car with me and said, 'Let's go look for him.' Just as we were about to leave, to our great relief, we saw a car with dad and his friend in it. All turned out well that night, but that was a typical day in our life."

There was a day, however, that didn't turn out so well. As is the case for everyone in our family, the day of March 22, 2006, was, and still remains, the most memorable day of Mohammed's memories of our time in our homeland. His reflections on that horrific day are meaningful in the sense that he, like my other brothers, witnessed everything . . . from the moment the bomb struck to the harrowing times that followed. Rather than reinterpret his words, I'll simply share them, just as he observed them, and just as he wrote them. He began,

> *There isn't a day that goes by where I don't remember March 22, 2006. That was the day Hisham's childhood was taken from him, and the day he could not hug me back. When the bomb fell, it felt like it was a movie. First, you black out, then you hear the ringing in your ears. The first moment I remember after the explosions was seeing my friend's bike on the ground. They were both gone. I saw Hisham on the ground and immediately ran towards him.*

> *My first instinct was to carry him inside the house since I was worried more bombs would fall. I saw him bleeding as soon as I laid him on the ground. I ran inside to see if I could get some cotton and try to stop the bleeding. He couldn't speak and was gasping for air. I realized as I was running back and forth to help Hisham that I was injured as well. My clothes were covered in blood.*

> *It was then that I heard our neighbors coming over to help us. I told them to get a car right away. We didn't have phones or ambulance services, because our area was on lockdown, which also meant cars going in and out of the*

area were at risk of being shot. Despite the restrictions, we scrambled to get into their car to get to the hospital. Hisham was put in the back of the car because it was suspected that he would not survive. When we arrived at the hospital, I saw my dad, who immediately ran towards me. I just told him to go see Hisham. My mom saw us and started crying. I still think of the horror my parents must have felt when they came into the emergency room to find three of their sons injured and bleeding lying next to each other.

Being a physician, my dad immediately went into doctor mode, tending to my brother's wounds and directing his staff. I am so grateful for the strength God gave to our dad.

After realizing the seriousness of Hisham's injuries, our dad walked into the room where we were being treated and announced he was taking our brother to Baghdad. I've never seen a father's anguish as I saw in our dad (our hero) at that moment. He was overwhelmed and in tears, but ever so determined. I think it was at that moment that I realized our lives were now going to be different.

When I first saw Hisham in the ICU, I couldn't believe my eyes. This was my little brother who we couldn't keep up with before because he had so much life, so much energy. He was on a ventilator and couldn't eat or speak or move a muscle. I broke down crying to the point where the staff thought there was something wrong with me. He still smiled when he saw me. That's how strong Hisham is.

I remember thinking to myself, he was a child who was stronger than war.

Both before and every day since that tragic day, Mohammed has been our big brother. Though my injuries were more severe, his life was just as disrupted. He, like my other brothers, was en route to fulfilling a well-planned life. And for him, like our brothers and our parents, those plans were destroyed on that tragic day.

Mustafa

Mustafa is my second-oldest brother. Miraculously, he was not injured by the bomb blast that shattered our lives that day. In one way, he was certainly fortunate to have avoided injury. In another way, however, he had to witness the brutality of what had happened and step up to help get my other brothers and me to the hospital in the immediate aftermath of the explosion.

Even though I am very happy he was not injured, I don't envy what he had to endure that day and the days that followed. As he reflected on the events leading up to that day, he was almost philosophical. He said, "It is amazing what one does to adjust to difficult situations. Living in Iraq during those times, the war was certainly present in our lives, but as long as it didn't intrude too much, we learned to live with it almost the way commuters in big cities learn to live with the inconvenience of traffic. On that day, however, everything changed."

He described how he was outside with his brothers and friends, doing nothing in particular, waiting for our afternoon school session to begin, when the bomb exploded next to our home.

"After the explosion," he said, "I opened my eyes and all I could see were my three brothers on the ground. My youngest brother, Hisham, was unconscious. My older brother, Mohammed, was injured, but not as severely as Hisham." He described how, after seeing my condition, Mohammed picked me up and began carrying me towards our house. Though Mustafa was not injured, he was certainly dazed by the blast.

He remembers our third brother, Ali, being conscious, but unable to stand. As Mohammed was attempting to help me, he said, he rushed to help Ali.

"We were all covered in blood and shouting and crying, still trying to comprehend what had just happened," Mustafa remembers. He reflected, "There we were, four school-aged brothers, ranging in age from 8 to 16, suddenly thrust into someone else's war that was not of our choosing."

He described the chaos and destruction of the scene, and feeling alone and helpless, and not knowing what to do next. He described how, almost immediately after the explosion, our neighbors rushed to our aid and put us all in a van to rush us to the hospital, he said. Mustafa was in the back of the van with me and my lifeless body. He described how he held me and kept whispering, "Everything will be OK; we will get you to the hospital. Everything will be OK." Knowing I was unconscious and probably could not hear him, Mustafa said, in reflecting back on those moments, he was perhaps uttering those words to give himself reassurance that I would be OK.

Mustafa described the scene at the hospital as utter chaos. The bomb had injured many people in the area, and the health care professionals were scrambling to treat them all. That is when he described how one of those health care professionals was our father, who was a physician at the hospital. He was already engaged in treating some of the other casualties who included, as I learned later, a friend of ours who had been killed by the explosion.

Coming from the room where our friend had died, my father's first awareness of our presence at the hospital was when he saw Mustafa and said, almost in a state of shock, "Why are you here?" There was terror in his voice, Mustafa said.

In response, he described how, as a 14-year-old boy who had just witnessed a horrific scene and seeing the terror in his father's eyes, he tried to maintain his composure without breaking down from the weight of it all. He told of how he tried to explain what had happened and pointed to my seemingly lifeless body, still unconscious and lying on the floor. My father immediately rushed to me, Mustafa said.

My father fortunately was able to detect a pulse and stop my bleeding, but I was still in a critical state. After doing all that could be done in the local hospital, and determining I would need additional treatment in Baghdad, Mustafa reflected on what that would mean for him. He said, "With my father transporting Hisham to Baghdad and the rest of us being left behind, I realized I was being thrust into a new position of responsibility. I was left by my father to take care of my two injured brothers and a heartbroken mother while he tended to Hisham. My older brother, Mohammed, was slightly injured, and my younger brother, Ali, more so from the blast and its complications."

He braced himself to remain calm while helping our grieving mother take care of my other two brothers, all while not knowing what was happening to me at the time. He reflected on how he, as a mere teenager, was forced to quickly learn to become a caregiver to his family under very agonizing and tragic conditions. I can only imagine what Mustafa must have been going through in those early hours after the explosion.

Five days later, he, my mother, and my other two brothers were able to join my father and me in Baghdad. Meanwhile, my neck injury, which had rendered me a quadriplegic, had been properly diagnosed. Further, I was on a ventilator. When I regained consciousness and could interact on a very limited basis, it was Mustafa and my other brothers who could make me smile. They would show me cartoons and joke with me, continuously looking for ways to engage me in those early days.

At the time, Mustafa described how he was curiously

intrigued by the nature of my treatment. He later shared that it was during his time of helping me that he realized he wanted to follow in my parents' footsteps and become a physician. He said, "I learned then that I wanted to dedicate my life to a profession of caring for those who were physically unable to do so themselves."

After being in Baghdad for a period of fifty-five days, we went to Jordan to continue my treatment. It was there, eighty-six days following my injury, that my tracheotomy was removed. Though I would continue to need more care, we were all beginning to feel better about my improvement.

By the time we moved to the United States, Mustafa had already had serious thoughts of becoming a doctor, but he said it was seeing how medicine was helping his brother that made him even more determined to enter the medical profession. As I continued to undergo further treatment, my brother continued to learn more about the advancements in stem cell research and other procedures that could help patients such as his brother. Those experiences eventually led him to volunteer at the Mercy Suburban Hospital and later at the Einstein Medical Center in the Philadelphia area. It was then and there that his commitment to medicine was solidified.

In the oddest of coincidences, it was the treatment I was undergoing, in Baghdad, in Jordan, and eventually in the United States, that brought Mustafa to his life's mission. During his experiences in those Philadelphia hospitals, he described how he found joy in helping others and talking to patients, as well as engaging with nurses and doctors. His delight in working with patients there, he said, brought him back to his memories of caring for his little brother.

As he reflected on the struggles we endured as a family and learned more about my progress and the advancements in medicine, he said, "I also learned more about myself."

Those struggles we endured not only made him stronger as a person, he said, but strengthened his passion to become a physician. "The more I had to stay strong to help my family persevere and help my little brother, the more I experienced the joy and gratification of helping others. And the more I had to be there for him when my parents were not present, the more I became confident in what I could do as a health care professional."

One of the many blessings that emerged from the tragedy and chaos of what happened to our family and to me, and the journey we were compelled to take, was the catalyst it provided to lead Mustafa to his life's work. His is a passion, perhaps born partly from my parents' professions and partly from my experience, but one nonetheless that gives me joy, pride, and admiration for my brother. He summarizes his extraordinary passion and determination, beautifully:

"I came to learn that medicine does not only cure diseases but also contributes to the well-being of families of those afflicted. Medicine brings hope to families, as it did to mine when we were affected in the aftermath of our horrific experience. Without doctors and medicine, we would have lost Hisham. He is now in a wheelchair with a spinal cord injury, but he still lives with the hope that medical research will help him recover someday.

"As are both of my parents, I am now in pursuit of becoming a doctor to keep that same hope alive, not only for Hisham, but for others like him. My goal is to instill the hope and the medical cures for those who are afflicted by diseases that are incurable today. Doctors can make profound changes in the lives of patients and their families, and I intend to do just that. Just as I have tried to do with my youngest brother since those years in the hospitals in Baghdad, Jordan, and here in the United States, I want to help a sick person smile again."

Ali

In 2014, some eight years after the bombing incident, Ali, the third of my three brothers, told his story of the bombing and its aftermath through an essay he wrote. His essay, in many ways, reflects the experiences and the thoughts of all of us.

As I prepared to tell my story, Ali shared his thoughts freely. He shared the pain and the disruption of our experience openly and without reservation. That's who Ali is. But rather than interpreting his thoughts through the filter of my own lens, I thought his essay captured them perfectly . . . and, in his own words.

Like Mustafa, Ali was drawn to the medical profession through our journey. And, like all of us, his experience and his perspective is a mixture of sadness, anger, frustration, and ultimately of love, commitment, and devotion to his family.

This was Ali's perspective in his own words, as he viewed our saga some eight years later:

A Frightening Childhood in a Beautiful Country

The air was filled with dust all around me. I could barely see anything. Moments later, I could see my brothers lying there bleeding, without any movement. War was all around us when I was growing up. I lived in Al-Ramadi, Iraq, with my mother, father, and three brothers: two older than me, Mohammed and Mustafa, and one younger than me, Hisham. Our relatives lived in Baghdad and Babylon, but we never felt like we didn't have relatives because our neighbors were like relatives to us.

When the war began in our country, the childhoods we knew of innocence and playfulness were lost. At first, we didn't know what was going on. But eventually, we became used to the presence of the soldiers, the planes, and the air raid alarms. When the war and the U.S. Army made it to our city, the house-to-house searches began. They started coming into our houses and taking prisoners.

There were other times when the soldiers started shooting without any apparent reason. There were curfews and times when we could not go to school because our roads were blocked, and we couldn't leave our house.

As the terror and disruption of war continued, many people began to leave the country. But we remained. This was our homeland. This was the country we loved.

On that tragic day, we were outside and heard the sound of a bomb. The next thing I knew, I was without feeling and unconscious. When I opened my eyes, the air around me was dusty and I could barely see anything. I saw my oldest brother, Mohammed, carrying Hisham toward our house. I saw my other brother, Mustafa, running to help me. The shock of it all prevented us from realizing that Hisham had a serious injury and that we each had many shrapnel wounds. Hisham was bleeding from his neck, and we were crying and shouting. When the neighbors heard us, they came with a car to take us to the hospital.

In the hospital I saw my friends crying. "What happened?" I asked. My brothers looked at me with a baffled look. It was then that my brother Mohammed told me, "Your best friend died." I was devastated. After I heard that, I fell to the ground, unconscious.

My parents were doctors working at this hospital, and both of them were shocked. My father instinctively went into "doctor" mode when he saw Hisham and his other sons lying in beds and on the floor, bleeding and unconscious. He moved quickly to stop Hisham's bleeding and began to care for him as the rest of us were being treated for our wounds. He soon concluded that the hospital in our city could not provide the care Hisham would require, and he decided he would take him to the hospital in Baghdad.

My mother, who was devastated by the events of that day, and my other two brothers and I remained behind in Ramadi, until we could rejoin Hisham and our father in the capital city five days later.

It is impossible for one's life not to be greatly affected by an event of this magnitude. You are subjected to experiences you would not ordinarily endure; you are forced to see things through the eyes of others; and, you are forced to grow up more quickly than those around you.

Later on in high school, I spent half a day, five days a week, at a hospital as a student intern. I spent two hours in a hospital classroom learning anatomy, physiology, and how to perform first aid and CPR. I learned to read X-rays. I did clinical rotations while shadowing different doctors. I learned the day-to-day management of a hospital, from every aspect. But most of all, I learned to see health care from the view of a patient. The engagement between health care professional and patient and bedside manner, I learned, was as important as all of the medical procedures.

The lessons for me, from our entire experience, were many. But two, in particular, stand out to me. First, I learned not to be afraid of anything. We experienced what has to be the most horrific experiences one can endure. It would be hard to imagine what could be more frightening.

Secondly, I learned to support my loved ones, no matter what. Much was taken from us that day. But we still had each other, and it was us, as a family, that would see us through the ordeal. I cannot imagine we would have made it, otherwise.

I once heard a quote that seemed to capture the hardships of our lives and the experiences we endured. It has remained with me as one of my favorites. It goes,

> *It has been said, that "time heals all wounds." I do not agree. The wounds remain. In time the mind, protecting its sanity, may cover them with scar tissue, and the pain may lessen. But it is never gone.*

> *—Anonymous*

This quote means a lot to me. After that incident my wounds remain. They are covered with scar tissue and don't hurt quite as much. But the pain that they caused me will be there forever. I am thankful, however, that my parents and brothers are still alive and that I can still see them as I do. I feel lucky to have the opportunity of a lifetime to live in this safe place as we do today.

Just as my brothers and I experienced that tragic day together, it is my brothers who have remained beside me every day since. The four of us are all older and far wiser since that day, but in their eyes, I am still their little brother. They look out for me and guide me just as they did when I was 8.

I have experienced many extraordinary blessings over the past ten-plus years. But none will surpass the love, support, and guidance I've received from my brothers.

PART III

Reflections and Reconciliation

Part III is a series of reflections of where we've come from, where we are today, both physically and emotionally, and observations and lessons we've learned along the way.

CHAPTER 14

A Religion Misunderstood

I**N THE TUMULTUOUS** years of the Civil Rights era in the United States, one of the factions that spoke out against racial discrimination called themselves Black Muslims. Under the leadership of individuals such as Elijah Muhammed, Malcolm X, and Louis Farrakhan, under the guise of Islamic teachings, the group justified militant acts to combat the oppression of Blacks in America.

As a result, in the eyes of many Americans, the words "Islam" or "Muslim" became synonymous with "Black Power," or the "Black Panthers," or other elements of violence or terrorism during the era. To many, "Muslims" meant one thing: terrorists.

On the international front, Israel, who has enjoyed strong support from America, was constantly engaged in conflicts with the Arab world. At stake was and continues to be the issue of the religious homeland of Palestine and the rights of the Arab world to their religious homeland. Names like Yasser Arafat and the Palestine Liberation Organization, or the PLO, still provoke images of terrorists and violence in the eyes of many.

The same is true for what was known as the Iranian hostage

crisis, when Iranian militants stormed the U.S. Embassy in Tehran in 1979 and held sixty-six Americans hostage for 444 days.

The fact that Iranians were engaged in their own version of the American Revolution was lost in the bedlam and chaos that followed. For years, Iran had been ruled by Mohammed Reza Pahlavi, the Shah of Iran, who was a despot and iron-fisted ruler. He was Iran's version of King George of England, and the Iranian people were like the American colonists who wanted their independence. But in this case, the despot ruler was supported by the American government, as he provided the U.S. access to Iran's oil. In protest, the revolutionaries stormed the U.S. consulate and took the employees (including three members of the Central Intelligence Agency) hostage.

This is not to justify the actions of the revolutionaries, but to point out the stigma of Muslims being a terroristic and violent religion.

That image was only further reinforced as the Americans went to war against the regime of Saddam Hussein in the 1990s. We all witnessed the violence by extremist groups such as al Qaeda or ISIS, which were associated with the Muslim religion. Then came the brutal attacks against America on 9/11. The bias toward Muslims and Arabs in general soon turned into an all-out uprising,

For many in America, Europe, and elsewhere, the stigma remains. The equation is simple:

Arabs = Muslims = militancy = violence.

That is the issue my family and the other approximately 1.8 billion Muslims around the world face every day. Islam is the fastest-growing religion in the world next to Christianity, and it constitutes roughly one-fourth of the world's population. One of the religion's cornerstones is promoting a peaceful coexistence. Yet it is perceived by a large population to be an instrument of war and violence.

"Radical Islamists" or "Muslim extremists," as they are referred to, make up less than a thousandth of 1 percent of Muslims worldwide. Yet because of their heinous actions, the remainder of those 1.8 billion suffer their stigma of being thought radical and dangerous.

In many ways, that rationale could be used to equate the violence of many so-called Christians. Timothy McVeigh, whose bomb killed 168 people in Oklahoma City, or Dylan Roof, who killed nine people in a church in Charleston, S.C., or Americans who have bombed Jewish synagogues or Islamic mosques, may view themselves as Christians, but they certainly did not exhibit the actions of the Christian faith.

In the same vein, those referred to as Muslim extremists or radical Islamic terrorists are not exhibiting actions of the Islamic faith.

The very term "Muslim extremist" is a contradiction in terms—an oxymoron, such as "military intelligence" or "jumbo shrimp."

The origins of my story do not begin with me or with my family, or even that fateful day in 2006. The beginnings go much further back. The American singer/songwriter Billy Joel wrote a song entitled "We Didn't Start the Fire." A recurring line in the lyrics is, "It's all been burning since the world's been turning . . . ."

That is certainly true of my country. Iraq and the countries of the Middle East are referred to as the "cradle of civilization." The region is also known as the birthplace of the various religions that have accompanied the birth of that civilization.

The Middle East has been in some form of turmoil for

centuries, and the roots of that turmoil, among other things, can ultimately be traced to religion.

Whereas Americans are predominantly Christians, the Iraqi people are predominantly Muslims. And just as there are different denominations in the Christian religion, such as Baptists, Methodists, Presbyterians, Catholics, and more, the Islamic faith basically consists of two denominations, Sunni and Shia.

All Christian denominations worship the same God, and they all believe in the same fundamentals of Christianity as put forth in the Bible. However, through the years, different people chose to interpret the Bible differently, resulting in groups splitting off to form different denominations within the Christian faith.

Those who characterize themselves as "moderate" Christians tend to recognize and respect the different beliefs of others, practicing somewhat of a "live and let live" philosophy. Those considered to be more extreme in their beliefs, however, feel differently. The more "fundamentalist" Christians, as they are referred to, have more difficulty accepting those differences, and in some cases, they will go to extremes to make their point. Those religious wars that have existed in the Christian faith have existed for centuries, dating back to the Crusades.

The same story can be told about the Islamic faith. If you substitute the name "Mohammed" for Jesus, and instead of the word "Bible," you insert the Koran, you see parallel stories. And the good news is, most moderates around the world, no matter their religion or who they worship, respect those differences.

The sad news is that it is the extremists in those religions that garner the headlines. They are the ones who take dramatic actions, including going to war over their beliefs. They are the ones prepared to kill in the name of God. That is true of the Islamic faith, just as it is in the world of Christianity or Judaism.

When you have one region of the world, such as the West, including Great Britain and the United States, who are dependent on oil, and you have another region that is rich in oil, you inevitably get political and military influences that invariably clash. When religions are thrown into that mix, such with Arab Muslims and Jews, those clashes become extreme. When Western countries, who have historically shown to exhibit the least geopolitical understanding of the Middle Eastern region, jump into the fray to protect their oil interests, all hell breaks loose.

Put it all together and you have a melting pot of conflicting interests, ripe for a perpetual state of turmoil. And it is that turmoil that has brought out the so-called Muslim extremists. Therein lies the paradox. Muslim extremists are certainly extreme, both in their beliefs and in their actions . . . but they're not Muslim. They may have been raised as Muslim, and they may even find some obscure elements in the Koran that, in some twisted interpretation, allows them to justify violence. But violence, in no way, is condoned or justified in the preachings of Islam.

And when you put Israel and the Jewish population into the mix, you get both political and religious clashes.

What you will find, in fact, is just the opposite. The Muslim religion, first and foremost, preaches peace. The first phrase you will hear when Muslims come together is "As-Salaam-Alaikum," the Arabic greeting meaning "Peace be unto you." It is not a phrase true Muslims take lightly. Whether in social gatherings or settings of worship, or other contexts, this is the greeting that true Muslims embrace and make every effort to live by.

Just like the Pledge of Allegiance or the Constitution in this country, that greeting embodies our faith and our way of life. The traditional response is just as meaningful: "Wa-Alaikum-

Salaam," meaning "And peace unto you," is the response you
will hear in informal gatherings, lectures, or sermons.

This greeting is one of the few linguistic conventions of
Eastern or "orthodox" Islam that the Nation of Islam has
retained since its origins. Further, there is clear verse in Quran
saying that for whoever kills a human being, it is the same as
killing all the humanity.

That is hardly the greeting you will hear from al Qaeda or
ISIS terrorists. While Arab extremists get all the press, most of it
negative and frightening to the uninformed, they unfortunately
are branded as Muslims.

That would be the equivalent of branding the KKK as
Christians, and therefore seeing them as representative of
the Christian faith. I don't think traditional, true Christians,
moderates or extremists, would advocate terrorist activities
against Blacks and Jews and Catholics.

What you find with Muslim extremists is what you can find
in any family: "I can fight my brother and call him names. But if
you fight my brother and call him names, you've got problems."

My father likes to point out that it isn't the religion of Islam
that is bad or problematic. The problem is that people who
don't know any better let themselves get brainwashed into
believing that our God is calling for them to take others' lives.
Our religion is a peaceful one, just like all of the world's great
religions. We hate it when people, Americans especially, get
tricked into believing that Muslims are a hateful people. That
couldn't be further from the truth. In fact, most Muslims, Iraqis
included, are some of the most peaceful, giving, warm, and
welcoming people alive.

So, what do we say to those people who question how we
can now live in the United States, given everything that has
happened to us? We say that like many other immigrants who
came here, all we aim to do is build better lives for ourselves.

While we have our grievances with the American government, we have nothing but love for American citizens. Soon after relocating here and becoming American citizens, we began to realize that the views of many American people are not the same as those of the American government. While there are religious biases everywhere, most Americans we met were no different from us . . . religious, God-fearing people, trying to live their lives and take care of their families. Though we may have different religious beliefs, the vast majority of Americans respect those differences. We are simply part of the American melting pot of Christians, Jews, Hindus, Muslims, or Buddhists from around the world, each choosing different ways to worship God, but members of the same world.

CHAPTER 15

A War of Brothers

DURING MY PLAYING time with the Philadelphia Power Player Hockey League, my family and I encountered a former U.S. Marine named Ed McEvoy. We learned that Ed had served in Iraq, and even Ramadi, during the time of the incident that caused my injuries. He, too, was playing in a hockey league affiliated with the Philadelphia Flyers professional hockey team, the Warrior Flyers.

During his tour of duty in Iraq, Ed had endured his share of injuries and was still receiving veterans medical benefits as a result.

We met at a time when my entire family was attending a hockey match, which gave all of us an opportunity to share our various experiences about those days in Iraq. We provided the perspective of being on the receiving end of America's invasion into our country, and Ed told us what it was like being an American combat Marine as part of the invaders.

In short, it was an extraordinary exchange. We all came to the same conclusions we had drawn from our previous experiences with American soldiers. Our countries were at war, but we had no personal animosities toward one

another as individuals. We were actually empathetic with
the predicaments our countries had subjected us to. He was
an American, serving his country and doing his job as best
he could. We were an Iraqi family with no grudge toward
Americans, but being subjected to the actions and the tragic
results of those actions by the U.S. Government.

Unknowingly, Ed became a part of our story when he
served as a U.S. Marine in Iraq at the time of the explosion.
He later became an extension of our family through our
mutual love of hockey and the Philadelphia Flyers.
From left are Mohammed, Ed, his fellow Warrior Jim Young,
my mom, Ali, my dad, and me in front.

He told us when he was first dispatched to Iraq, he, like
all of us, had been monitoring the news and the rumblings of
war. And he, like all of us, had heard on the news that Saddam
Hussein had been stockpiling weapons of mass destruction, and
was an evil tyrant who needed to be deposed. He knew of the
Iraqi insurgents who were swarming the country and had to be

eliminated. He, like us, had heard all the political propaganda from both sides, but he was in a special position to be privy to the American side in much greater detail.

He said that going into the war, he felt anxious, yet ready to answer his nation's call.

As a gung-ho, 19-year-old Marine, he said, he felt invincible and ready to do whatever the U.S. Marine Corps asked of him, and without question, He told me this not as a bloodthirsty, brainwashed Marine, "as we were commonly perceived," but as a young Marine concerned about the safety of the world.

Later, after he had arrived in the country, he had his first in-depth view of the Iraqi people.

Prior to joining the Marine Corps, Ed told us, he had never left the United States, or even traveled far beyond the Philadelphia area. He said he had no idea what to expect. He told us how most movies that involved the Middle East portrayed the region as hostile towards Americans. The unknown was a little worrisome to him, but he said the training he had received prior to arriving in our country was reassuring.

The training reaffirmed that the majority of Iraqis were good people and not a threat. He said much of his military training prior to being deployed to Iraq was about our culture and our customs. The training, he told us, emphasized how the U.S. soldiers should view themselves not as conquerors, but as liberators.

He then described to us that first day when he arrived in our country.

"As we made our way into Iraq on March 20, 2003, we were greeted with little resistance, and I was immediately introduced to the Iraqi people. I found them to be kind and friendly, but just like me, they were scared, worried, and confused, just as I would be if in their shoes. Some were angry, and I understood why. Though there were language differences, words were not necessary to tell us how they felt. Their emotions spoke clearly."

Ed described in vivid detail his experiences of the horrors of war. He said he learned quickly that movies of war do not tell the whole story. "You expect casualties on both sides," he said, "but the emotional toll is something that you could never imagine. Seeing my fellow Marines and coalition troops killed or wounded weighs on me till this day. But seeing innocent civilians killed or maimed, and families decimated, is something I'll never be able to forget.

The U.S. military employed local Iraqis to assist in their rebuilding efforts. This is Ed with the foreman and intermediary of the Iraqi work crew, Hussein. In this photo, Hussein was ironically wearing a shirt he had acquired brandishing the name of the bank that had employed Ed back in the U.S., the Commerce Bank.

"Knowing that these people were just going about their business and trying to live their lives, and for them to suffer the way they did, was very emotional for me. Seeing the pain and sadness on the faces of the Iraqi people led me to think about the same for the families of fallen U.S. servicemembers. Death is hard enough to deal with, but adding the suffering and sadness of what their families go through brings it to a whole new level."

The more Ed talked of his experiences, the more I realized that we were both casualties of the war. I and my family suffered immeasurably because of the war. But in a different way, so had he. Though we experienced it from different sides, and in dramatically different ways, we were all casualties. As he continued to talk about his experiences, I found myself wondering, if both sides suffered the way he described, then who were the winners?

As he continued talking, he spoke of the sinister way that war changes people. When you're in an environment in which you could be alive one minute and dead the next, you forego the natural light side of your human emotions and go to a much darker place. Your more lighthearted feelings such as joy, laughter and love, he said, give way to the more sinister feelings of fear, mistrust, and even hate.

"I've seen the most caring and empathetic people," he continued, "become numb due to the stress of war. The way they talked to others, the way they looked at others, and the way they thought about them—something changes in people when fear sets in. They go into survival mode, and it's as if nothing else matters."

He recalled how, in the opening days of the war, militants would use white flags to show that they were surrendering to U.S. troops, and then attack them when the soldiers let their guard down. "Lives were lost," he said. "We realized we could be attacked anywhere by anybody. Our emotions and our tactics changed. Not knowing who was good or bad, or who was legitimately surrendering, we were in survival mode. And in survival mode, everyone is the enemy. The individual smiling at you yesterday could be the one shooting at you today."

Though he could not speak for other Americans who had experienced more severe trauma and hardships than he, Ed said he was thankful to have served under the leaders he did, because they placed an emphasis on controlling these types of negative emotions and thoughts. He said he was constantly reminded, "You can still be humane and stay alert at the same time."

As a show of its partnership with the Iraqi people, the U.S. flew the flag of Iraq on its installations, Due to the unavailability of official flags, Hussein, the Iraqi foreman, arranged to have a homemade flag, which was proudly flown as the "official" flag. Ed proudly displays that flag in his office today. Pictured from left are Ed, Hussein, and Ed's fellow Marine Dave Kallam in 2005.

A friend once told me, "The first time you visit a foreign country, you realize how different the people are from you. The second time, however, you begin to realize how similar they are to you." As Ed continued to talk, I realized he had begun to experience that phenomenon.

He described how, after being in the country and working and living with Iraqis, the color of their skin and their broken English accents became a non-factor. They were all human beings like him, caught up in the same tragedy.

That is the great paradox of war. Even the bravest of soldiers and the fiercest of combatants are, at their core, not enemies. In many instances, they can't remember what they are fighting for. In the midst of the most heinous carnage, they are often able to discover the humanity in their fellow man.

That is what Ed was able to do. Even though his government told him he was there to fight the forces of evil, through it all, he found humanity.

From left are Hussein, Ed, and fellow worker, Cookie.

"During my second deployment," he told us, "I had the opportunity to interact with Iraqis on a daily basis. These were men who were hired by the U.S. government to preform construction, demolition, and other jobs on our base. During some down time, I would escort them on to our base from the main gate. Many of them spoke broken English and were able to communicate. Those who spoke no English would communicate with us through their foreman, Hussein, who spoke fluent English.

"We eventually became friends with Hussein and his workers. We joked around constantly, laughing at each other's expense, and we shared personal interests, gripes, and backgrounds. I told them of America, and they told me of Iraq. Pretty soon, we were no longer Americans and Iraqis; we were colleagues.'

Ed, with his Iraqi crew at his going-away celebration in 2005.
All proudly display New York Yankees baseball caps.

"We knew of each other's families, and I looked forward to seeing them every single day. But after a short time, our friendship became dangerous. Local insurgents had two enemies: Americans, and Iraqis who befriended Americans. They began to identify Iraqis who were working on our base and would ambush and kill them as they made their way home. We lost several Iraqi friends that way. They either suffered that fate or never returned out of fear of suffering that fate. Either way, we lost friendships who were never heard from again."

Ed was emotional about his military experience, especially in describing his final day in our country.

"My last day in country was bittersweet. I was excited to return home to my family, but I was sad to leave my good friends behind. Knowing the situation of them and their families and the fact that they lived under threat from insurgents, there was no guarantee of safety for them or their families. This goodbye was a true goodbye. We would most likely never see each other, or hear from each other, ever again.

"I still miss these guys to this day and think about them often. I keep pictures of them in my home, office, and on my social media. I can still hear their voices and their laughs and see their smiles. I hope and pray that each one of them is doing well and living a prosperous life."

Meeting Ed and getting his perspective on the war was invaluable for us. The war, without question, changed our lives forever, and as we listened to him tell his story, I had the feeling that it had a similar impact on him. It was a very heartwarming experience for all of us, but in some ways a sad remembrance of that time in our lives.

Unknowingly, Ed became a part of our story when he was a U.S. Marine serving in Iraq at the time of my injuries. He later became part of our story through our mutual love of hockey and the Philadelphia Flyers hockey team. Ed wrote of those experiences, both in Iraq, and in meeting us. He wrote the following:

> *Meeting Hisham and his family and hearing Hisham's story brought up a lot of emotions from my experience in Iraq. I often wonder about the many people I met there. Especially the people who were wounded, or the families I'd seen grieving.*
>
> *Where are they now? How are they doing? What quality of life do they have, if any? All these thoughts keep me up at night and sidetracked during the day. These people were complete strangers, and in the eyes of many, were our enemy. But we became friends.*
>
> *Seeing how Hisham has progressed over the years, his mindset—his outlook—is truly inspirational. His quest to share his story to promote peace is so courageous, and admirable on so many levels. I am extremely grateful that I was able to cross paths with Hisham and his family, and who would have thought that hockey would be the reason for it?*

Our family is grateful for meeting Ed. He put a human U.S. face on a war of violence that is generally executed by faceless people. Though we were on different sides of that terrible conflict, we found ourselves in agreement on the tragedy of war and the deadly human toll it takes on individuals, families, and nations.

It is ironic that the very men and women that are dispatched to go off and fight a nation's war are the ones that come home as the most outspoken voices for peace.

Thank you, Ed, for joining us in our quest for the one thing we have pursued and advocated for since that day in March of 2006.

CHAPTER 16
A Message of Peace

SPENDING MUCH OF the last decade in a wheelchair and living in a country I never would have imagined, it is in inevitable that I occasionally reflect back on the events of that day and ponder the "what ifs."

What if Saddam Hussein had never invaded Kuwait? What if the Bush Administration were not convinced that he had weapons of mass destruction? What if Saddam had complied with the sanctions that were imposed upon him? What if the Americans had not launched the bomb that destroyed our home? What if my brothers and I had been in school that morning? The questions are endless.

Any one of those "what ifs" would have avoided the entire tragic episode that altered our lives forever, and we would be back in our home in Ramadi fulfilling our father's vision for us. While my focus has been to look forward toward the future and not dwell on the past, those questions invariably seep back into my mind, as I'm sure they do with the rest of my family, and millions of Iraqi people.

The biggest "what if" of all of them, however, is the one that has haunted us for centuries and obviously still does:

What if countries were dedicated to resolving their differences peacefully as opposed to resorting to war and violence?

My father, abiding by our Muslim faith, reminds us that resolution to conflicts can be achieved, and should be, through peaceful means. He reminds us that war is never the answer. He has told us, "Any crazy person can start a war, but it needs all the wise people around the world to try to stop it."

He talks about how it's going to take decades to rebuild the nation of Iraq after the years of fighting and the subsequent takeover of parts of the country by religious extremists.

My father has always been focused on his faith and his family. But, given what has happened to us, he has added a third focus. He is now determined to be a voice that educates others about the true consequences of war, as well as our need to find resolution to conflicts through peaceful means.

This and other wars have had devastating effects on so many people, in so many ways. Consider the people whose country was invaded. Consider the American soldiers who had to leave their own homelands and families to fight. Consider their families and the disruption to their lives. Consider the soldiers who lost their lives. Their promise of a future was taken from them, as it was for their families. Consider the lives of the thousands of innocent civilians who were caught in the crossfire. Consider the massive property damage and destruction, which, for us, included sacred religious shrines that embodied the birth of our civilization.

All of this because the leaders of two countries couldn't agree.

Is this where we are in the twenty-first century? Have we learned nothing from the death and destruction caused by wars throughout history? Are we no smarter today, in this age of unprecedented innovation and technology, than we were in the fifteenth century?

We have taken the arts of communication, medicine, and manufacturing to extraordinary lengths. We have the technology to allow our cars to drive themselves. We can turn the lights or the oven in our house on or off remotely from another country. I, as a quadriplegic, have the ability to read, write, solve problems, get an education, and navigate to any place on Earth, all without leaving this chair that confines me.

Yet we seem not to have advanced at all in the art of solving problems peacefully among nations.

My father and mother struggle greatly with the fate that has befallen me. I know there are times when they want to ask members of the United States government if they are able to sleep at night knowing that their actions have caused others so much hardship. They speak to families still living in Iraq and trying to live their lives the best they can under horrific circumstances.

Though I no longer have the use of my arms and legs, I thank God every day that I am still alive and have such a wonderful family who takes care of me. Others, however, have not been so lucky. Many of our fellow countrymen have died as a result of the war in my homeland. These include men, women, and children, soldiers and civilians.

On the day of the bombing, one of the neighborhood boys who I was close with lost his life. He tried to run to a neighborhood store as the blood came pouring from his body. Unfortunately, he never made it out of that store, succumbing to his mortal wounds right then and there. As he continued running towards his home to see his family, he fell to the floor and met his fate.

My mother has spoken to families we knew back in Iraq who once thrived and lived decent and prosperous lives, but now sadly feel that they no longer have a future in their home country. The parents are starting to lose hope, and their children are starting to do poorly in school. We have not just lost the present generation, but generations to come because of this war.

The violence begets more violence.

As despair turns to hopelessness, hopelessness turns to extremism. One of the reasons that many resort to religious extremism, my father is convinced, is because they feel they have nothing to lose. They have no jobs. Maybe they lost their families to war. They might simply need the money. After all, why else would someone willingly volunteer to kill others or themselves or both? Still others might join extremist groups out of revenge, perhaps to avenge friends or loved ones who were killed during the war.

We have suffered mightily as a result of what we and our friends and families back in Iraq have experienced. The pain and the sadness are pervasive.

But the greatest sadness of it all is that it was avoidable!

The phrase "war is hell" is a common and overused expression. From watching historical footage of World War II and the Holocaust and movies about war, such as *Saving Private Ryan*, my family and I can relate to the expression all too well. However, considering what we have gone through over the past decade, the phrase does not capture the full magnitude of war.

When lives and families are destroyed because two or more countries can't agree on an issue, or because the ruler or maniacal dictator of a country wants something that someone else possesses, it goes beyond hell. It adds a new dimension to the description.

When someone doesn't think like you, or believe the same things you do, or look like you, conflicts invariably arise. Or when someone has something that you want, or when someone has offended you or has done something or said something to insult your honor, violence is always a potential result.

Are these not problems that can be solved without resorting to violence? Families have demonstrated their ability to do so. Corporations have demonstrated the ability to do so. Communities have shown their ability to do so.

And yet, many countries cannot.

Even with mechanisms, such as the United Nations or the International World Court, that are in existence for this very purpose, nations seem to bypass them at will and resort to the most destructive form of problem solving. It seems that the entities with the greatest capacity to inflict damage and destruction with the might of their great militaries are the very entities least able to resolve their differences.

It appears, as my father has suggested, if we're going to achieve some level of success in promoting peace over war, it will have to begin at the grassroots level. What we need is a movement, not unlike the anti-war movement in this country during the Vietnam War. That movement didn't begin in Washington. It began in community centers, college campuses, and neighborhood gatherings around the country. Meetings turned to marches. Marches turned to protests. Protests turned to media coverage, and *then* the movement found its way to Washington!

From California to Maine to Florida, the movement eventually got the attention of members of Congress, senators, and the president, who saw their voters in the streets, demanding change.

Where is that movement today?

We are even better equipped today than we were in the 1960s to spread the word. Today, we have social media and other technologies that allow us to have community discussions nationally, even worldwide. We have the technology to voice our opinions instantly and collectively.

In addition to rebuilding our lives here in America and

finding the health care that will give me back the full use of my body, our mission is to serve as an instrument of peace. We continue to seek, invite, and welcome any opportunity to tell our story, and we offer our experiences and hard-earned lessons in support of that purpose.

The world awaits a better solution.

Epilogue

IT'S BEEN OVER a decade since that fateful day in 2006.

It seems like an eternity since we left our home in Ramadi and went virtually around the world in search of the miracle that would correct the paralysis I suffered from that bomb. Yet, in other ways, it seems like yesterday.

The images of that warm morning, being outside playing with my brothers, are burned into my memory—as is the eerie whistling noise we heard just before the explosion that shattered our home, our lives, and my mobility.

Being the youngest of four brothers and being eight years old at the time, I had grown accustomed to being looked after by my older brothers. I was used to them cautioning me and guiding me about what to do and what not to do. I was used to them admonishing me when I failed to heed their warnings. I was also used to them teasing me and joking with me, and sometimes even taunting me. They were what you would want if you were the youngest of four brothers, guiding you, protecting you, and taking care of you.

After that day, that phrase took on a new meaning. My brothers could not protect me from the explosion of the American bomb, but they certainly took care of me. From getting me back to our home after the explosion hit, to getting me to the hospital and eventually into the care of my parents, they were there.

When my father moved me the to the hospital in Baghdad, my mother and my brothers were right behind us. When we moved from Baghdad to Jordan, once again, they were right behind us. And when we made the biggest decision of our lives to relocate to America, they, as did I, had tremendous reservations about coming to the U.S., but they were there!

They had their own lives to live. They had their educations to complete. They had careers to consider. But, that became secondary. Looking after their little brother came first, even if it meant moving to the other side of the world.

When I was in the Baghdad hospital, my oldest brother, Mohammed, was really great. I later learned that he would often stay awake at night to watch over me and make sure everything was OK. Further, I learned that on many nights, Mustafa slept on the floor near the foot of the bed, just to help my father care for me during the night. He would wake up with the slightest noise that I made to make sure I was OK.

I guess it's just what good big brothers do.

They adjusted their lives for me.

I kept waiting for them to complain. I kept waiting for them to grow tired of their own lives being put on hold to accommodate the welfare of their little brother. Yet, they never did . . . not once. Instead, as they did before that horrible day, they were there to guide me, encourage me, and make me laugh when I needed to laugh most.

That is true even today. They continued with their educations. They are pursuing their own lives, their own careers, but they continue to look after their little brother, who is now 21 years of age. They still guide me. They still make me laugh. And sometimes when I think I've learned something new and am the smartest person in the room, they still rib me and remind me I'm not.

Today, my brothers are achieving all my father could have envisioned for them. Mohammed is an engineer for a multinational firm. Mustafa is now completing his residency training in internal medicine at Henry Ford Hospital in Detroit. And Ali is in his final year of medical school.

Our family at my brother Mustafa's graduation from Lake Erie College of Osteopathic Medicine in 2019. From left are my dad, Mustafa, my mom, me, Ali, and Mohammed. It was a very proud day, especially for my parents.

While my journey has been a wild one, and not the one that I would have envisioned for myself, my brothers were right there with me, and I'll never forget them for it.

Outside of my condition as a quadriplegic and being

confined to a wheelchair, however, it is perhaps my parents who have had to make the biggest adjustment of all. Like me, my brothers were young when our lives were totally disrupted. The young have a greater capacity to adjust and adapt than do adults who are already established in their lives and routines. My parents were well into their careers as medical professionals in the local hospital. They were well into the task of raising their family and building their vision of a family compound.

As I reflect on that terrible day, I realize how hard it must have been for my parents during this time. I mean, clearly, I was going through my own difficulties, but I don't have children, so I have no idea what it is like to see your child in such a grave situation. It must truly be awful.

Their lives were well established, only to be totally disrupted.

Since that day, my father has been on a decades-long quest to find a solution to my condition, and at the same time, had to navigate our move to the U.S. and reestablish his career. My mother has totally put her career as an eye specialist on hold to become a fulltime caregiver for me.

Like with my brothers, there were many nights when I wondered, at what point will they grow weary of the existence that has befallen them and want their lives back? At what point will they say enough is enough? The answer, I have come to learn, is never. It is their tireless devotion to my wellbeing that has taught me more than I will ever learn through my spiritual teachings about faith and unconditional love.

Today, my father keeps the piece of shrapnel that was lodged in my neck as a keepsake. He says it's crazy that a little piece of metal like that could destroy families. It also serves as a reminder of not only the life we once had, but that from which we came, more than a decade ago.

If I never walk again, it is my dream to make them proud of

me and feel gratified that all their sacrifice and hard work was worth it.

For me, the decade-long journey has clearly been a challenge. From the moment that explosion hit, mine was no longer a life of innocence, going to school with my brothers and playing with my friends. No longer was it a life of being able to stand up and walk into the kitchen to eat dinner with my family, feed myself, or dress myself.

From that fateful day, March 22, 2006, my life went from being one of freedom, self-sufficiency, and unbridled joy, to one of being totally dependent on my family and caregivers, and a confinement to a wheelchair that is my constant companion.

Mine has been a life filled with bouts of deep depression, the never-ending "what ifs," and the struggles to find a reason to wake up in the morning. Fortunately, it has also been a life of faith, determination, eternal optimism, self-discovery, accomplishment, and purpose.

To borrow a phrase from the marketing world, I have had to "re-brand" myself. I had no choice. Fortunately, with the aid of technology, I have choices I would have never had years earlier. I can't walk and I cannot move my arms, but with the technological capabilities of this chair, there's not much else I cannot do. I can read, I can write, I can communicate, I can move about, all on my own.

Back when I was confined to a hospital bed, I always thought that getting out of the hospital and getting back to some sense of normalcy would be the easy part. But it wasn't. There were many more difficulties ahead. I could no longer do things like pick up a pen or type on a keyboard. How could I possibly continue my education? Technology has taken care of most of that.

I still wait for the medical technology that will give me back my ability to walk and give me the use of my arms and hands.

The shrapnel from the blast that day fractured my C5 and C6 vertebrae and injured my spinal cord, which is the basis of my paralysis. The technology to correct that is what I wait for. In the meantime, I continue to live my life.

I am frequently asked how I remain so upbeat, so positive, so motivated. The answer is generally threefold: my faith, which was instilled in me as a young boy by my parents; the love, support, and encouragement of my family and friends; and the technology that enables me to experience most everything a person needs to live a fulfilling life.

When people tell me my attitude is "heroic" or inspiring, I truly appreciate that. But, in the spirit of full disclosure, being constantly inspiring to others can sometimes be a burden. I still have my down days. I still occasionally get depressed. I still get envious of others who have the ability to walk or throw a football.

I still have trouble dealing with the fact that the day of the bombing was the last time I ever saw my childhood home. It was truly heartbreaking to realize that I would be leaving our neighbors and friends behind.

I recently received my associate's degree at Montgomery County Community College here in Pennsylvania. I celebrated with my family, friends, and classmates at the commencement exercise. It was a joyful day to be proud of what I had accomplished. But, oh, what I would have given to have been able to walk across that stage to receive my diploma!

But, despite those occasional lapses into the world of envy, "what ifs," and regrets, I continue to live my life looking forward and not backward. A day with nature usually helps get me back on the right track.

Next on my agenda is continuing my education and obtaining my four-year degree. And, who knows, maybe after that I'll obtain my graduate degree.

My ultimate goal is to be of help to others. Whether they face physical limitations like mine, or emotional limitations, or challenging social circumstances, there are many people who need our help. And given my experience, I believe I can be of help. So, as I look at career choices, it is the helping professions that motivate me most.

My other goal, like my father, is to be a messenger of peace. We have lived firsthand the ravages of war. And as elusive as it sometimes seems, we know that peaceful resolution is achievable, among people, among communities, and among nations.

White, black, red, or brown; Muslim, Christian, Hindu or Jew; Democrat or Republican; conservative or progressive; we are all more alike than different. We all want basically the same thing . . . to raise our families in a peaceful society and have access to the same opportunities as others.

From TED talks, to social media, to community advocacy, I believe our family and I have a story to tell that can help further those causes. And we continue to build toward those opportunities.

Today, we are thousands of miles and more than a dozen years removed from that fateful day. Instead of being in Ramadi, living out the original vision of my father, we are now enjoying a modified and revived version of that vision as part of the multicultural fabric of greater Philadelphia, Pennsylvania, in the United States.

In many respects, what happened on that day in 2006 seems like a lifetime ago. In other respects, it seems like it happened yesterday. In any case, my family and I are now embarked on our new lives as Americans, and we are looking forward to sharing our story . . . one of destruction and consequences of war, and one of peace.

*   *   *

Acknowledgments

I WOULD LIKE TO express my deepest gratitude to my parents and my brothers as this book would not have been possible without their support.

I am immensely grateful to have met and worked with our ghostwriter G. Ross Kelley who was a wonderful person.

Special thanks goes to the publishing company Gatekeeper press for all the good work they did.

Special thanks to all my friends and colleagues who encouraged me to pursue writing this book and motivated me to keep going.

I would like to also express my deepest thanks to all those who have touched my life since the day of my injury. I am truly thankful to every single one of you and for all that you have done for me.

Lastly, I would like to thank everyone who has followed my story through social media or elsewhere and who has invested the time to read my book to learn my story.

Made in the USA
Middletown, DE
23 March 2022